Pleasures of
NATURE

A LITERARY ANTHOLOGY

Pleasures of
NATURE

A LITERARY ANTHOLOGY

selected by
Christina Hardyment

THE BRITISH LIBRARY

CONTENTS

Fire 97

Deep Thinking 195

Afterword 218

☙ Introduction

A Description of a great Variety of Animals and Vegetables: viz. Beasts, Birds, Fishes, Insects, Plants, Fruits, and Flowers. Extracted from the most considerable Writers of Natural History; and adapted to the Use of all Capacities, but most particularly for Entertainment.
Thomas Boreman, *Compendium of Zoology*, 1744

The world is made up of four elements: Earth, Air, Fire and Water. This is a fact well known even to Corporal Nobbs. It's also wrong. There's a fifth element, and generally it's called Surprise.
Terry Pratchett, *The Truth*, 2000

Surveying literary approaches to all things natural has proved an even more endless quest than gathering together their ideas about gardens and about food, the subjects of my first two anthologies in this series. 'How deep is the ocean? How high is the sky?' I found myself humming as the piles of poets and novelists on the library floor mounted. I was reminded of Arthur Ransome's description of compiling an anthology of friendship with the help of his wife Ivy:

> We walk up and down, smoking and observing the shelves, as you would watch a crowd in which you might have friends. Book after book reminds us of something which should find its place in the shadowy volume that is building in the air.

At last I thought of an ancient and most respectable framework in which Nature could (after a fashion) be tidied: that of the Four Elements. Earth, Air, Fire, Water: couldn't most observations be fitted under these heads? Not quite, and many fitted more than one. Two more categories emerged: one that I originally called Pure Fun, but decided to rename Surprise in honour of the late, great, Terry Pratchett; and Deep Thinking, a seemly place for passages that stop one in one's tracks and engender a sense of wonder.

Earth includes the quiet mysteries of Wordsworth's ancient yews and Stuart Edward White's 'high, wild country of wonder', as well as extreme phenomena such as the 'incessant woo, woo, woo' of the Singing Sands discovered on the island of Eigg by the Victorian geologist Hugh Miller, the 'dreadful canopy' of Gordale Scar in Yorkshire wondered at by Thomas Grey, and the underground 'arched cathedral' explored by Thomas Lovell Beddoes. Then there are particularly earthbound creatures: a hedgehog and two tortoises. Lilian Bowes Lyon's 'Snow Hare' is far from earthbound, but her 'light lady of the sorrows' uses the earth as her springboard.

Air is the home of rainbows, winds and mists, the 'tremendous voice' of James Thomson's thunder, and the 'livid flame' of his lightning. Leonardo da Vinci analyses the varying blues of atmosphere: smoky grey, azure, profoundly dark. Edward Thomas observes a 'candied violet sky' at twilight, and Henry Alford revels in a 'shroud of dazzling mist' at the summit of Skiddaw. Air is the domain of birds and insects. Tennyson's eagle 'falls like a thunderbolt', and Audubon's 'laughs like a maniac'. William Canton chuckles at an 'old, ungodly rogue' of a crow, and Gilbert White recognises different birds by their flight. Lousia Budgen admires a 'brilliant bevy' of moths, and Emerson a bumblebee: 'zig-zag steerer, desert cheerer'.

Fiery phenomena invade all the elements of course, be they volcanoes (observed at Pompeii by Pliny, and at Krakatoa by R M Ballantyne), 'phosphorescent billows' as whales' tails lash the sea in *Moby-Dick*, or Robert Service's 'wild and weird and wan' Northern Lights dancing in the polar sky. Thomas Hardy likens the great bonfire lit on the heath in *The Return of the Native* to ancient funeral pyres; Laurence Binyon's garden bonfire is an elegy for the passing year. And there is a phoenix, which, Bartholomew Anglicus tells us, crawls into a nest 'of right sweet-smelling sticks', which is set on fire by the sun.

Having Surprise as a fifth element made it easy to find a home for the curiosities that any composer of an anthology lights upon.

There are the cunning dragons that Pliny describes elephants battling against mightily, the geese born from barnacles solemnly recorded by William Harrison, and Lewis Carroll's nonsensical bread-and-butterfly. There are also teasing pokes at amateur naturalists in George Crabbe's eager young wife struggling with 'learned words, … urged with force, / Panduriform, pinnatifid, premorse', and Margaret Gatty's suggestions for suitable wear for exploring rock-pools: 'A ladies' yachting costume has come into fashion of late, which is perhaps as near perfection for shore-work as anything'.

In the Deep Thinking section, God recurs: as a 'vast Chain of Being' for Alexander Pope, in the changing seasons for Henry Vaughan, in the form of Space for Coleridge, jokingly in Rupert Brooke's piscine 'Heaven'. The Japanese poet Bashō reads Buddhist poems under the moon, Robert Louis Stevenson wanders the bird-enchanted highlands in 'a trance of silence', Thomas Hardy finds hope in a gaunt and aged thrush. The pioneer environmentalist Aldo Leopold reminds us that 'in wildness is the salvation of the world', and the physicist Chet Raymo gazes at the stars from a dark hillside, listening and watching 'for the tingle in the spine'.

There is much to comfort, but also much to dread. I came away from reading centuries of natural observations with the sad realisation that we are taming and tidying the once fecund world around us so thoroughly that we risk everything. In our gardens, birds, bees and hedgehogs disappear in the face of pesticides. The rockpools on our beaches are all but deserted. In South America, Africa and Asia, forests shrink unimaginably quickly, and round the globe the oceans are being invaded and polluted for profit. As we reach greedily for the stars, let's stop a while and remember Gilbert White's tortoise, digging himself into the ground with a movement that 'little exceeded the hour hand of a clock', and the tall old shepherd in the Lakeland Hills who, Harriet Martineau tells us, 'has trod upon rainbows'.

Earth

Of all that earth has been or yet may be, all that vain men imagine or believe, or hope can paint or suffering may achieve, we descanted.

Percy Bysshe Shelley, 'Julian and Maddalo: *A Conversation*', 1824

❧ A Spirit of Growth

Leonardo da Vinci (1452–1519) recorded his ideas about the world in a series of notebooks. His beautifully expressed thoughts on the Earth itself occur in his 'Treatise on Water'. This translation is from Edward MacCurdy's 1871 edition of the notebooks.

The grass grows in the fields, the leaves upon the trees, and every year these are renewed in great part. So then we may say that the earth has a spirit of growth, and that its flesh is the soil; its bones are the successive strata of the rocks which form the mountains; its cartilage is the tufa stone; its blood the springs of its waters. The lake of blood that lies about the heart is the ocean. Its breathing is by the increase and decrease of the blood in its pulses, and even so in the earth is the ebb and flow of the sea. And the vital heat of the world is fire which is spread throughout the earth; and the dwelling place of its creative spirit is in the fires, which in divers parts of the earth are breathed out in baths and sulphur mines, and in volcanoes, such as Mount Etna in Sicily, and in many other places.

✍ The Work of the Omnipotent

John Speed (1552–1629) was a historian and cartographer. This dramatic description of the landslide near Much Marcle, Herefordshire, is from his Theatre of the Empire of Great Britaine *(1610). Kinnaston Chapel's bell was later unearthed and hung in the tower of Homme House.*

But more admirable was the work of the Omnipotent, even in our own remembrances, and year of Christ Jesus 1571, when the Marcley Hill in the East of this Shire, rouzed itself out of a dead sleep, with a roaring noise removed from the place where it stood, and for three days together travelled from her first site, to the great amazement and fear of the beholders. It began to journey upon the seventh day of February, being Sunday, at six of the clock at night, and by seven in the next morning had gone forty paces, carrying with it sheep in their cotes, hedge-rows, and trees; whereof some were overturned, and some that stood upon the plain, are firmly growing upon the hill; those that were East were turned West; and those in the West were set in the East: in which remove, it overthrew Kynaston Chapel, and turned two highways near an hundred yards from their usual paths formerly trod. The ground thus travelling, was about twenty six acres, which opening itself with rocks and all, bare the earth before it for four hundred yards space without any stay, leaving that which was pasturage in place of the tillage and the tillage overspread with pasturage. Lastly, overwhelming her lower parts, mounted to an hill of twelve fathoms high, and there rested herself after three days travel, remaining His mark, that so laid hand upon this rock, Whose power hath poised the Hills in his Balance.

❧ Terrestrial Heaven

John Milton (1608–1674) conjured up the natural imagery in his blank verse epic Paradise Lost *(1664) from memory, as his sight had completely failed by 1651. In this passage from Book VIII, Satan mourns his expulsion from enjoyment of the good things of the Earth.*

O Earth, how like to Heav'n, if not preferr'd
More justly, seat worthier of Gods, as built
With second thoughts, reforming what was old!
For what God, after better, worse would build?
Terrestrial Heav'n, danced round by other Heavens
That shine, yet bear their bright officious Lamps,
Light above light, for thee alone, as seems,
In thee concentring all their precious beams
Of sacred influence: As God in Heaven
Is centre, yet extends to all, so thou
Centring receiv'st from all those orbs; in thee,
Not in themselves, all their known virtue appears
Productive in Herb, Plant, and nobler birth
Of creatures animate with gradual life
Of Growth, Sense, Reason, all summed up in Man.
With what delight could I have walked thee round
If I could joy in aught – sweet interchange
Of hill and valley, rivers, woods and plains,
Now land, now sea, & shores with forest crowned,
Rocks, dens, and caves; but I in none of these
Find place or refuge; and the more I see
Pleasures about me, so much more I feel
Torment within me, as from the hateful siege
Of contraries; all good to me becomes
Bane...

ᘉᕈ Peevish Elfe

Richard Braithwaite (1588–1673) wrote this enchanting description of that very earthbound creature the hedgehog in A Strange Metamorphosis of Man, Transformed into a Wilderness *(1634). I have left it in its original spelling, as it adds so much to its charm.*

The Hedgehog is a right Urchin and a peevish Elfe, that cannot bee medled with at no hand. He is a whole fort in himselfe, hee the Governor, his skin the walls, his prickles the Corpes de guard. He is very jealous and suspitious by nature, so that he never takes his rest, till hee have set the watch. He hath a drawbridge to collect himselfe with at his pleasure, especially when he stands upon his guard, so as it were impossible to make any breach into him … Hee is all comb, though not to kemb with, which hath no teeth but to mischiefe with, and therefore is no friend from the teeth outward, while every tooth is a very sting. He is but a milksop yet, and a very suckling, who will hang on the speens of every Cow, which therefore makes him cry so like a child. He cannot brag much of his gentry, whose father was a Boare, his mother a Sow, himselfe a Pigge, and all begot under a hedge. If there bee any such place as Hoggs Norton is, where Piggs play on the Organs, it is surely with them; who have such a squeeking cry with their wind instruments. What his flesh is to eat, I know not, but I should think, hee that should eat him whole, were as good have a burre in his throat. They say his flesh is as good and as tender as a Rabbet, but this I am sure, their furre is nothing neere so gentle. As the Fox hath his hole, so hath he his bush, from whence there is no getting him forth, till he be fired out. Hee is no great medler himselfe, nor loves to bee medled with, nor any that is wise, I think, will teyze with him, who knowes how touchy hee is. For my part, if I stumble not on him, I will have nothing to do with him.

❧ Wave-swollen Earth

William Strode (c. 1601–1645) was a Devonshire-born poet, who spent most of his life in Oxford, and won a reputation as 'a most florid preacher' after being ordained. This description evokes the dramatic contours of the downs around Uffington.

When Westwall Downs I gan to tread,
Where cleanly winds the green did sweep,
Methought a landskip there was spread,
Here a bush and there a sheep:

The pleated wrinkles of the face
Of wave-swollen earth did lend such grace,
As shadowings in Imag'ry
Which both deceive and please the eye.

The sheep sometimes did tread the maze
By often winding in and in,
And sometmes round about they trace
Which milkmaids call a Fairy ring:

Such semicircles have they run,
Such lines across so trimly spun
That shepherds learn when e'er they please
A new Geometry with ease.

The slender food upon the down
Is always even, always bare,
Which neither spring nor winter's frown
Can ought improve or ought impair:

Such is the barren Eunuch's chin,
Which thus doth evermore begin
With tender downs to be o'ercast
Which never comes to hair at last.
Here and there two hilly crests
Amidst them hug a pleasant green,
And these are like two swelling breasts
That close a tender fall between.

Here would I sleep, or read, or pray
From early morn till flight of day:
But hark! a sheep-bell calls me up,
Like Oxford college bells, to sup.

❧ Dreadful Canopy

Thomas Gray (1716–1771) spent most of his life writing poetry in scholarly seclusion in Cambridge, but in later years he enjoyed travelling in the North of England in search of dramatic landscapes.

October 13, 1769: Settle … is a small market-town standing directly under a rocky fell. There are not a dozen good-looking houses, the rest are old & low with little wooden porticoes in front. My inn pleased me much (tho' small) for the neatness & civility of the good Woman that kept it, so I lay there two nights, & went to visit Gordale-scar. Wind NE: day gloomy and cold. It lay but six miles from Settle, but that way was directly over a fell, and it might rain, so I went round in a chaise the only way one could get near it in a carriage, which made it full thirteen miles; and half of it such a road! But I got safe over it so there's an end, and came to Mallham (pronounce it Maum), a village in the bosom of the mountains seated in a wild and dreary valley: from thence I was to walk a mile over very rough ground. A torrent rattling along on the left hand.

On the cliffs above hung a few goats; one of them danced and scratched an ear with its hind foot in a place where I would not have stood stock still for all beneath the moon. As I advanced the crags seemed to close in, but discovered a narrow entrance turning to the left between them. I followed my guide a few paces, and lo, the hills opened again into no large space, and then all farther away is barred by a stream, that at the height of above 50 feet gushes from a hole in the rock, and, spreading in large sheets over its broken front, dashes from steep to steep and then rattles away in a torrent down the valley.

The rock on the left rises perpendicular with stubbed yew-trees and shrubs staring from its side to the height of at least 300 feet; but those are not the things: it is that to the right under which you stand to see the fall that forms the principal horror of the place. From its very base it begins to slope forwards over you in one block and solid mass without any crevice in its surface, and overshadows half the area below with its dreadful canopy. When I stood at (I believe) full four yards distance from its foot, the drops which perpetually distil from its brow, fell on my head, and in one part of the top more exposed to the weather there are loose stones that hang in the air and threaten visibly some idle spectator with instant destruction. It is safer to shelter yourself close to its bottom, and trust to the mercy of that enormous mass which nothing but an earthquake can stir. The gloomy uncomfortable day well suited the savage aspect of the place, and made it still more formidable.

⟨⟩ The Old Tortoise

Gilbert White (1720–1793) was exceptionally fond of the aged tortoise that he first came across in 1770 and inherited from his aunt in 1780. In a letter to his friend Daines Barrington (12 April, 1772), he describes how 'Timothy' dug into the earth to hibernate. Then over thirty years old, the tortoise (in fact a female) died in 1793.

While I was in Sussex last autumn my residence was at the village near Lewes, from whence I had formerly the pleasure of writing to you. On the first of November I remarked that the old tortoise, formerly mentioned, began first to dig the ground in order to the forming its hybernaculum, which it had fixed on just beside a great tuft of hepaticas. It scrapes out the ground with its fore-feet, and throws it up over its back with its hind; but the motion of its legs is ridiculously slow, little exceeding the hour-hand of a clock; and

TESTUDO PARDALIS, *Bell.*

suitable to the composure of an animal said to be a whole month in performing one feat of copulation. Nothing can be more assiduous than this creature night and day in scooping the earth, and forcing its great body into the cavity; but, as the noons of that season proved unusually warm and sunny, it was continually interrupted, and called forth by the heat in the middle of the day; and though I continued there till the thirteenth of November, yet the work remained unfinished. Harsher weather, and frosty mornings, would have quickened its operations. No part of its behaviour ever struck me more than the extreme timidity it always expresses with regard to rain; for though it has a shell that would secure it against the wheel of a loaded cart, yet does it discover as much solicitude about rain as a lady dressed in all her best attire, shuffling away on the first sprinklings, and running its head up in a corner. If attended to, it becomes an excellent weather-glass; for as sure as it walks elate, and as it were on tiptoe, feeding with great earnestness in a morning, so sure will it rain before night. It is totally a diurnal animal, and never pretends to stir after it becomes dark. The tortoise, like other reptiles, has an arbitrary stomach as well as lungs; and can refrain from eating as well as breathing for a great part of the year. When first awakened it eats nothing; nor again in the autumn before it retires: through the height of the summer it feeds voraciously, devouring all the food that comes in its way. I was much taken with its sagacity in discerning those that do it kind offices; for, as soon as the good old lady comes in sight who has waited on it for more than thirty years, it hobbles towards its benefactress with awkward alacrity; but remains inattentive to strangers. Thus not only 'the ox knoweth his owner, and the ass his master's crib,' (Isaiah I, 3) but the most abject reptile and torpid of beings distinguishes the hand that feeds it, and is touched with the feelings of gratitude!

❧ A Natural Temple

William Wordsworth (1770–1850) celebrated the deep-rooted and ancient endurance of the yew tree at Lorton in Allerdale, and of the 'fraternal Four of Borrowdale' – now sadly reduced to three, but still awesomely atmospheric.

There is a Yew-tree, pride of Lorton Vale,
Which to this day stands single, in the midst
Of its own darkness, as it stood of yore:
Not loathe to furnish weapons for the Bands
Of Umfraville or Percy ere they marched
To Scotland's heaths; or those that crossed the sea
And drew their sounding bows at Azincour,
Perhaps at earlier Crecy, or Poictiers.
Of vast circumference and gloom profound
This solitary Tree! a living thing
Produced too slowly ever to decay;
Of form and aspect too magnificent
To be destroyed. But worthier still of note
Are those fraternal Four of Borrowdale,
Joined in one solemn and capacious grove;
Huge trunks! – and each particular trunk a growth
Of intertwisted fibres serpentine
Up-coiling, and inveterately convolved,
Nor uninformed with Fantasy, and looks
That threaten the profane; a pillared shade,
Upon whose grassless floor of red-brown hue,
By sheddings from the pining umbrage tinged
Perennially; beneath whose sable roof
Of boughs, as if for festal purpose decked
With unrejoicing berries, ghostly Shapes
May meet at noontide: Fear and trembling Hope,
Silence and Foresight, Death the Skeleton

And Time the Shadow; there to celebrate,
As in a natural temple scattered o'er
With altars undisturbed of mossy stone,
United worship; or in mute repose
To lie, and listen to the mountain flood
Murmuring from Glaramara's inmost caves.

ᴄ❧ A Subterranean City

Thomas Lovell Beddoes (1803–1849) was fascinated by the occult and the macabre. His fantastical poem 'A Subterranean City' reflects contemporary geological and paleontological discoveries of wonders under the surface of the earth.

I followed once a fleet and mighty serpent
Into a cavern in a mountain's side
And, wading many lakes, descending gulphs,
At last I reached the ruins of a city,
Built not like ours but of another world,
As if the aged earth had loved in youth
The mightiest city of a perished planet,
And kept the image of it in her heart,
So dream-like, shadowy, and spectral was it.
Nought seemed alive there, and the bony dead
Were of another world the skeletons.
The mammoth, ribbed like to an arched cathedral,
Lay there, and ruins of great creatures else
More like a shipwrecked fleet, too vast they seemed
For all the life that is to animate:
And vegetable rocks, tall sculptured palms,
Pines grown, not hewn, in stone; and giant ferns,
Whose earthquake-shaken leaves bore graves for nests.

Fig. 8

fig. 2

fig.24 neer Keinsham.

fig.

.19.

fig. 18   fig 23   22.   fi.17   Fig.16   Fig. 15   Fig. 14   Fig 6

Fig. 1

.13   Fig 4   Fig. 3

Fig. 5ª

fig

Fig 10   Fig. 11   fig. 20

Fig

Fig. 27   fig. 21

❧ Golden Desert

In Jane Eyre *(1847), Charlotte Brontë's heroine finds solace on the moor when she flees from Thornfield Hall after her shocking discovery of the attic existence of Rochester's mad wife.*

I struck straight into the heath; I held on to a hollow I saw deeply furrowing the brown moorside; I waded knee-deep in its dark growth; I turned with its turnings, and finding a moss-blackened granite crag in a hidden angle, I sat down under it. High banks of moor were about me; the crag protected my head: the sky was over that …

I touched the heath: it was dry, and yet warm with the heat of the summer day. I looked at the sky; it was pure: a kindly star twinkled just above the chasm ridge. The dew fell, but with propitious softness; no breeze whispered. Nature seemed to me benign and good; I thought she loved me, outcast as I was …

I saw ripe bilberries gleaming here and there, like jet beads in the heath: I gathered a handful and ate them with the bread. My hunger, sharp before, was, if not satisfied, appeased by this hermit's meal. I said my evening prayers at its conclusion, and then chose my couch.

Beside the crag the heath was very deep: when I lay down my feet were buried in it; rising high on each side, it left only a narrow space for the night-air to invade. I folded my shawl double, and spread it over me for a coverlet; a low, mossy swell was my pillow. Thus lodged, I was not, at least – at the commencement of the night, cold …

Next day, Want came to me pale and bare … I got up, and I looked round me. What a still, hot, perfect day! What a golden desert this spreading moor! Everywhere sunshine. I wished I could live in it and on it. I saw a lizard run over the crag; I saw a bee busy among the sweet bilberries. I would fain at the moment have become bee or lizard, that I might have found fitting nutriment, permanent shelter here. But I was a human being, and had a human being's wants: I must not linger.

❧ The Singing Sands of Laig

Hugh Miller (1802–1856), best known for The Old Red Sandstone *(1841) was a self-taught Scottish geologist who had a remarkable knack of finding striking metaphors and similes in his writings.* The Cruise of the Betsey *(1857) described a summer rambling in the Hebrides, where he discovered strange marvels on the island of Eigg. Yes, it looks long, but persevere; it is astonishing.*

We pass on towards the north. A thick bed of an extremely soft white sandstone presents here, for nearly half a mile together, its front to the waves, and exhibits, under the incessant wear of the surf, many singularly grotesque combinations of form. The low precipices, undermined at the base, beetle over like the sides of stranded vessels. One of the projecting promontories we find hollowed through and through by a tall rugged archway; while the outer pier of the arch, – if pier we may term it, – worn to a skeleton, and jutting outwards with a knee-like angle, presents the appearance of a thin ungainly leg and splay foot, advanced, as if in awkward courtesy, to the breakers.

But in a winter or two, judging from its present degree of attenuation, and the yielding nature of its material, which resembles a damaged mass of arrow-root, consolidated by lying in the leaky hold of a vessel, its persevering courtesies will be over, and pier and archway must lie in shapeless fragments on the beach. Wherever the surf has broken into the upper surface of this sandstone bed, and worn it down to nearly the level of the shore, what seem a number of double ramparts, fronting each other, and separated by deep square ditches exactly parallel in the sides, traverse the irregular level in every direction. The ditches vary in width from one to twelve feet; and the ramparts, rising from three to six feet over them, are perpendicular as the walls of houses, where they front each other, and descend on the opposite sides in irregular slopes.

The iron block, with square groove and projecting ears, that receives the bar of a railway, and connects it with the stone below, represents not inadequately a section of one of these ditches, with its ramparts. They form here the sole remains of dykes of an earthy trap, which, though at one time in a state of such high fusion that they converted the portions of soft sandstone in immediate contact with them into the consistence of quartz rock, have long since mouldered away, leaving but the hollow rectilinear rents which they had occupied, surmounted by the indurated walls which they had baked. Some of the most curious appearances, however, connected with the sand-stone, though they occur chiefly in an upper bed, are exhibited by what seem fields of petrified mushrooms, of a gigantic size, that spread out in some places for hundreds of yards under the high-water level. These apparent mushrooms stand on thick squat stems, from a foot to eighteen inches in height; the heads are round like those of toadstools, and vary from one foot to nearly two yards in diameter. In some specimens we find two heads joined together in a form resembling a squat figure of eight, of what printers term the Egyptian type, or, to borrow the illustration of M'Culloch, 'like the ancient military projectile known by the name of double-headed shot'; in other specimens three heads have coalesced in a trefoil shape, or rather in a shape like that of an ace of clubs divested of the stem. By much the greater number, however, are spherical. They are composed of concretionary masses, consolidated, like the walls of the dykes, though under some different process, into a hard siliceous stone, that has resisted those disintegrating influences of the weather and the surf, under which the yielding matrix in which they were embedded has worn from around them. Here and there we find them lying detached on the beach, like huge shot, compared with which the greenstone balls of Mons Meg are but marbles for chil-dren to play with; in other cases they project from the mural front of rampart-like precipices, as if they had been showered into them by the ordnance of some besieging battery, and had stuck fast in the mason-work. Abbotsford has been described as a romance in stone and lime; we have here, on the shores of Laig, what seems a wild but agreeable tale, of the extravagant cast of 'Christabel', or the 'Rhyme of the Ancient Mariner', fretted into sandstone. But by far the most curious part of the story remains to be told.

The hollows and fissures of the lower sandstone bed we find filled with a fine quartzose sand, which, from its pure white colour, and the clearness with which the minute particles reflect the light, reminds one of accumulations of potato-flour drying in the sun. It is formed almost entirely of disintegrated particles of the soft sandstone; and as we at first find it occurring in mere handfuls, that seem as if they had been detached from the mass during the last few tides, we begin to marvel to what quarter the missing materials of the many hundred cubic yards of rock, ground down along the shore in this bed during the last century or two, have been conveyed away. As we pass on northwards, however, we see the white sand occurring in much larger quantities, – here heaped up in little bent-covered hillocks above the reach of the tide, – there stretching out in level, ripple-marked wastes into the waves, – yonder rising in flat narrow spits among the shallows. At length we reach a small, irregularly-formed bay, a few hundred feet across, floored with it from side to side; and see it, on the one hand, descending deep into the sea, that exhibits over its whiteness a lighter tint of green, and, on the other, encroaching on the land, in the form of drifted banks, covered with the plants common to our tracts of sandy downs. The sandstone bed that has been worn down to form it contains no fossils, save here and there a carbonaceous stem; but in an underlying harder stratum we occasionally find a few shells; and, with a specimen in my hand charged with a group of bivalves resembling the existing conchifera of our sandy beaches, I was turning aside this sand of the Oölite, so curiously reduced to its original state, and marking how nearly the recent shells that lay embedded in it resembled the extinct ones that had lain in it so long before, when I became aware of a peculiar

sound that it yielded to the tread, as my companions paced over it. I struck it obliquely with my foot, where the surface lay dry and incoherent in the sun, and the sound elicited was a shrill, sonorous note, somewhat resembling that produced by a waxed thread, when tightened between the teeth and the hand, and tipped by the nail of the forefinger. I walked over it, striking it obliquely at each step, and with every blow the shrill note was repeated. My companions joined me; and we performed a concert, in which, if we could boast of but little variety in the tones produced, we might at least challenge all Europe for an instrument of the kind which produced them. It seemed less wonderful that there should be music in the granite of Memnon, than in the loose Oölitic sand of the Bay of Laig. As we marched over the drier tracts, an incessant woo, woo, woo, rose from the surface, that might be heard in the calm some twenty or thirty yards away; and we found that where a damp semi-coherent stratum lay at the depth of three or four inches beneath, and all was dry and incoherent above, the tones were loudest and sharpest, and most easily evoked by the foot.

❧ The Silence of the Hills

To experience to the full the profound peace of Cumbria's high hills, Harriet Martineau (1802–1876) recommended a walk up from Rydal to Fairfield via Nab Scar in her Guide to the Lakes *(1855).*

Perhaps a heavy buzzard may rise, flapping, from its nest on the moor, or pounce from a crag in the direction of any water-birds that may be about the springs and pools in the hills. There is no other sound, unless it be the hum of the gnats in the hot sunshine. An old shepherd has the charge of four rain gauges which are set up on four ridges, – desolate, misty spots, sometimes below and often above the clouds. He visits each once a month, and notes down what these gauges record; and when the tall old man, with his staff, passes out of sight into the cloud, or among the cresting rocks, it is a striking thought that science has set up a tabernacle in these wildernesses, and found a priest among the shepherds. That old man has seen and heard wonderful things: – has trod upon rainbows, and been waited upon by a dim retinue of spectral mists. He has seen the hail and the lightnings go forth as from under his hand, and has stood in the sunshine, listening to the thunder growling, and the tempest bursting beneath his feet. He well knows the silence of the hills, and all the solemn ways in which that silence is broken.

The stranger, however, coming hither on a calm summer day may well fancy that a silence like this can never be broken. Looking abroad, what does he see? The first impression probably is of the billowy character of the mountain groups around and below him. This is perhaps the most striking feature of such a scene to a novice; and the next is the flitting character of the mists. One ghostly peak after another seems to rise out of its shroud; and then the shroud winds itself round another. Here the mist floats over a valley; there it reeks out of a chasm: here it rests upon a green slope; there it curls up a black precipice. The sunny vales below look like a paradise,

with their bright meadows and waters and shadowy woods, and little knots of villages. To the south there is the glittering sea; and the estuaries of the Leven and Duddon, with their stretches of yellow sands. To the east there is a sea of hilltops. On the north, Ullswater appears, grey and calm at the foot of black precipices; and nearer may be traced the whole pass from Patterdale, where Brothers Water lies invisible from hence. The finest point of the whole excursion is about the middle of the cul-de-sac, where, on the northern sides, there are tremendous precipices, overlooking Deepdale, and other sweet recesses far below. Here, within hearing of the torrents which tumble from those precipices, the rover should rest. He will see nothing so fine as the contrast of this northern view with the long green slope on the other side, down to the source of Rydal Beck, and then down and down to Rydal Woods and Mount. He is now 2,950 feet above the sea level; and he has surely earned his meal.

⚕ Green Groweth the Grass

William Morris (1834–1896) first published his Norse fantasy The Story of the Glittering Plain, or The Land of Living Men *as a serial in the* English Illustrated Magazine *(vol. 7, 1890), then in 1891 made it the first book he printed at his own Kelmscott Press. This 'snatch of song' appears in Chapter XVIII.*

Fair is the world, now autumn's wearing,
And the sluggard sun lies long abed;
Sweet are the days, now winter's nearing,
And all winds feign that the wind is dead.

Dumb is the hedge where the crabs hang yellow,
Bright as the blossoms of the spring;
Dumb is the close where the pears grow mellow,
And none but the dauntless redbreasts sing.

Fair was the spring, but amidst his greening
Grey were the days of the hidden sun;
Fair was the summer, but overweening,
So soon his o'er-sweet days were done.

Come then, love, for peace is upon us,
Far off is failing, and far is fear,
Here where the rest in the end hath won us,
In the garnering tide of the happy year.

Come from the grey old house by the water,
Where, far from the lips of the hungry sea,
Green groweth the grass o'er the field of the slaughter,
And all is a tale for thee and me.

⒝ A Mighty Polypus Mouth

Sabine Baring-Gould (1834–1924) was inspired to write his Winefred: A Story of the Chalk Cliffs *(1900) by accounts of the great Bindon land-slide at Seaton in 1839. Jane Marlby is warned to abandon her cottage by a labourer.*

No wind was stirring. The moment was that of the turn of the tide. At a distance of half a mile from the shore the surface of the water heaved like the bosom of a sleeper in rhythmic throb. There were no rollers, no white horses.

But nearer land the sea was boiling. Volumes of muddy water surged up in bells as from a great depth, and spread in glistening sheets, that threw out wavelets which clashed with the undulations of the tide. Moreover, there appeared something like a mighty monster of the deep, ruddy brown, heaving his back above the water.

'That which is coming in is sweet water,' said the man. 'One of our chaps has ventured down and tasted it. It is not the fountains of the deep that are broken up, but the land springs are feeding the ocean. Did you ever witness the like?'

'Yes,' said Jane, 'there was something of the kind took place, but only in a small way, before the crack formed when my old cottage was ruined.'

'Exactly, missus. And there is going to happen something of the same sort here, but on a mighty scale, to which that was but as nothing. Where it will begin, how far it will extend, all that is what no mortal can guess. Now you know why I have been sent to tell you to clear out as fast as you can.

She returns to the house, but Oliver Dench, the villain of the piece, ties her up and steals her stash of gold. She struggles to the window:

Looking out she saw Dench standing irresolute – as one dazed. She saw something more. At that moment the house swayed like a ship. The surface of the land broke up, and seemed transmuted into fluid, for in one place it heaved like a mounting billow, and in another sank like the trough of a wave. It was to Jane, peering through the little window as though she were looking at a tumbling sea through the porthole of a cabin. Again the house lurched, and so suddenly and to such an acute angle, that Jane fell from the table. ...

Her daughter Winefred is looking for her, as the villagers gaze in horror.

She was taking the path that led to the cottage, when she was arrested by a loud and general cry that ran from west to east; and immediately she heard a strange rending sound as of thick cloth ripped asunder ... At once was seen a jagged fissure running like a lightning-flash through the turf, followed by a gape, an upheaval, a lurch, then a sinkage, and a starring and splitting of the surface. In another moment a chasm yawned before their eyes, three-quarters of a mile long, torn across the path, athwart hedges, separating a vast tract of down and undercliff from the mainland, and descending into the bowels of the earth.

Winefred was caught by the shoulder and hurled back. It was not safe to stand near the lip of this hideous rent, for that lip broke up and fell in masses into the abyss. Cracks started from it, or behind it, and widened, and whole blocks of rock and tracts of turf disappeared. The surface beyond the chasm presented the most appalling appearance. It was in wild movement, breaking up like an ice-pack in a thaw. It swayed, danced, fell apart into isolated blocks, some stood up as pillars, some bent as horns, others balanced themselves, then leaned forward, and finally toppled over and disappeared ... A wide tract of land, many acres in length, had separated from the main body and was sliding seaward in a tilted position. At the same moment from out the sea rose a black ridge, like the back of a whale, but this drew out and stretched itself parallel to the fissure.

An awed silence had fallen on the spectators as they held their breath to watch the progress of the convulsion that was changing the outline of the coast and transforming its appearance.

But suddenly a cry was heard, and next moment some one was

seen running on the sloping and still sliding mass. It was not Jane Marley. It was a man carrying a carpet-bag. For some time none could make out who he was; but the Captain of the Excise, who had a glass, exclaimed that he was Dench, the ferryman. Oliver appeared to be panic-stricken to such an extent as to have almost lost his senses. Seeing the crowd he ran towards it, along the path from the cottage till he came upon the gap that was rapidly widening and dividing him at every moment farther from the mainland. He seemed as though on board a vessel that was being swept out to sea, and frantically strove to escape from her to those who stood on the wharf observing him. Down into the separating chasm eyes looked, but could not make out the bottom; the depth contained a tossing mass of crumbled chalk and erupted pebble, with occasional squirts of water, some two or three hundred feet below the surface on the land side. It was like a mighty polypus mouth that had opened and was chewing and digesting its food in its throat and belly.

❦ Ancient and Dark

Edward Thomas (1878–1917) had a close affinity with the Wiltshire landscape. His poem 'The Combe', written in December 1914, described the scarp edge north of the Marlborough Downs.

The Combe was ever dark, ancient and dark.
Its mouth is stopped with brambles, thorn, and briar;
And no one scrambles over the sliding chalk
By beech and yew and perishing juniper
Down the half precipices of its sides, with roots
And rabbit holes for steps. The sun of Winter,
The moon of Summer, and all the singing birds
Except the missel-thrush that loves juniper,
Are quite shut out. But far more ancient and dark
The Combe looks since they killed the badger there,
Dug him out and gave him to the hounds,
That most ancient Briton of English beasts.

ᘒ Little Titan

D H Lawrence (1885–1930) became fascinated by tortoises while he was living in Italy, and published six poems about them in Tortoises *(1921). 'Baby Tortoise', the first, is a nice contrast to Gilbert White's description of the aged 'Timothy' earlier in this section.*

You know what it is to be born alone,
Baby tortoise!
The first day to heave your feet little by little
    from the shell,
Not yet awake,
And remain lapsed on earth,
Not quite alive.

A tiny, fragile, half-animate bean.

To open your tiny beak-mouth, that looks as if
    it would never open,
Like some iron door;
To lift the upper hawk-beak from the lower base
And reach your skinny little neck
And take your first bite at some dim bit of
    herbage,
Alone, small insect,
Tiny bright-eye,
Slow one.

To take your first solitary bite
And move on your slow, solitary hunt.
Your bright, dark little eye,
Your eye of a dark disturbed night,
Under its slow lid, tiny baby tortoise,

So indomitable.

No one ever heard you complain.

You draw your head forward, slowly, from your
    little wimple
And set forward, slow-dragging, on your four-
    pinned toes,
Rowing slowly forward.
Whither away, small bird?

Rather like a baby working its limbs,
Except that you make slow, ageless progress
And a baby makes none.

The touch of sun excites you,
And the long ages, and the lingering chill
Make you pause to yawn,
Opening your impervious mouth,
Suddenly beak-shaped, and very wide, like some
    suddenly gaping pincers;
Soft red tongue, and hard thin gums,
Then close the wedge of your little mountain
    front,
Your face, baby tortoise.

Do you wonder at the world, as slowly you turn
    your head in its wimple
And look with laconic, black eyes?
Or is sleep coming over you again,
The non-life?

You are so hard to wake.

Are you able to wonder?
Or is it just your indomitable will and pride of
    the first life
Looking round
And slowly pitching itself against the inertia
Which had seemed invincible?

The vast inanimate,
And the fine brilliance of your so tiny eye.

Challenger.

Nay, tiny shell-bird,
What a huge vast inanimate it is, that you must
    row against,
What an incalculable inertia.

Challenger.

Little Ulysses, fore-runner,
No bigger than my thumb-nail,
Buon viaggio.

All animate creation on your shoulder,
Set forth, little Titan, under your battle-shield.

The ponderous, preponderate,
Inanimate universe;
And you are slowly moving, pioneer, you alone.

How vivid your travelling seems now, in the
    troubled sunshine,
Stoic, Ulyssean atom;

Suddenly hasty, reckless, on high toes.

Voiceless little bird,
Resting your head half out of your wimple
In the slow dignity of your eternal pause.
Alone, with no sense of being alone,
And hence six times more solitary;
Fulfilled of the slow passion of pitching through
    immemorial ages
Your little round house in the midst of chaos.

Over the garden earth,
Small bird,
Over the edge of all things.

Traveller,
With your tail tucked a little on one side
Like a gentleman in a long-skirted coat.

All life carried on your shoulder,
Invincible fore-runner.

The Cross, the Cross
Goes deeper in than we know,
Deeper into life;
Right into the marrow
And through the bone.

✺ Snow Change

*Lilian Bowes Lyon (1895–1949) lived in Ridley Hall, Northumberland,
and the northern landscape informs both her poems and her novels. She was
a first cousin of Queen Elizabeth the Queen Mother. Hares are not exactly
earthbound, but they do spring off it, and no anthology of nature can omit
them. 'The White Hare', published in 1928, is a magical description of a
hare in winter.*

At the field's edge
In the snow-furred sedge,
Couches the white hare;
Her stronghold is there

Brown as the seeding grass
In summer she was,
With a creamed belly soft as ermine;
Beautiful she was among vermin.
Silky young she had,
For her spring was glad;
On the fell above
She ran races with love.
Softly she went
In and out of the tent
Of the tasselled corn;
Till the huntsman's horn
Raised the bogy death
And she was gone, like breath.

Thanks to her senses five
This charmer is alive:
Who cheated the loud pack,
Biting steel, poacher's sack;

Among the steep rocks
Outwitted the fanged fox.
And now winter has come;
Winds have made dumb
Water's crystal chime;

In a cloak of rime
Stands the stiff bracken;
Until the cold slacken
Beauty and terror kiss;
There is no armistice.
Low must the hare lie,
With great heart and round eye.

Wind-scoured and sky-burned
The fell was her feet spurned
In the flowery season
Of her swift unreason;
Gone is her March rover;
Now noon is soon over;
Now the dark falls
Heavily from sheer walls
Of snow-cumbering cloud,
And Earth shines in her shroud.
All things now made
That were in love's image made.

She too must decrease
Unto a thorny peace,
Who put her faith
In this flesh, in this wraith.
A hoar habit borrows
Our light lady of sorrows,
Nor is her lot strange;
Time rings a snow-change.

Air

The inner – what is it?
if not intensified sky,
hurled through birds and deep
with the winds of homecoming

Rainer Maria Rilke, 'Shut Out from
the Law of the Stars', 1934

ᑌ Winds A-whoop

'Nature was to Virgil no unmeaning apparition, but a glorious scroll, over-written with messages full of divinity,' runs an endpaper note by Herbert Bland, husband of Edith Nesbit, and former owner of my battered Victorian edition of the Works of Virgil *(70–20 BC). 'Nowhere is this more evident than in the Georgics, which aimed to set the dignity of labour above the glory of war.' R D Blackmore, author of* Lorna Doone, *was the translator of this passage from the first Georgic.*

The stars and storms autumnal shall I sing,
When days decrease and summer suns decline,
How men must watch? Or when the close of spring
Descends in showers tempestuous and malign;
When tufts of harvest ruffle o'er the plain,
And on the green stalk swells the milky grain?
Oft have I seen – what time the fanner bold
Would guide the reaper through his realms of gold.
And strow the swath of barley – on them swoop
The warring fury of all winds a-whoop:
Up from the roots the pregnant corn is riven,
Swept up on high, and dash'd across the heaven,
Soaring away go reeds, and sheaves, and all,
In buoyant circles riding the black squall.
And oft the squadrons of great waters form.
And ocean-clouds amass the solemn storm:
Down falls the vaulted welkin, and the rain,
A rushing deluge, dashes ploughs and grain;
The dikes are fill'd; the hollow rivers roar;
The sea lies hissing on its panting shore.
In midmost night of clouds the Father stands,
And holds the thunder hurtling in his hands;
Whereat the vast earth lies a-quake and pale.

The lions fly, the hearts of nations quail:
He, with the shaft of fire, in dust hath strawn
Athos, or Rhodope, or high Ceraun:
With double fury rush the winds and rain,
While woods and shores wail to the hurricane.
In fear of this, observe the month and star,
Where Saturn's freezing planet roves afar,
To which of heaven's broad trackways shall retire,
In circling travel the Cyllenian fire.

☞ The Wind Beneath Their Wings

De Arte Venandi cum Avibus *was a popular medieval manual compiled by Frederick II, Holy Roman Emperor (1194–1250) in 1245. This translation, published as* The Art of Falconry *in 1943, is by Albert Casey Wood.*

With prophetic instinct for the proper time to migrate, birds as a rule anticipate the storms that usually prevail on their way to and from a warmer climate ... they are usually able to choose a period of mild and favouring winds. North winds, either lateral or from the rear, are favourable, and they wait for them with the same sagacity that sailors exhibit when at sea ... The calls of migrating cranes, herons, geese and ducks may be recognised flying overhead even during the night ... they are the call notes of one or more birds talking to their fellows. They understand wind and weather so thoroughly that they know when meteorological conditions are favourable and are likely to remain so long enough to enable them to reach their intended haven. Weak fliers postpone their journey until they are sure of a prolonged period of good weather sufficient for their migrating venture...

The order of migration may be summed up as follows: not all shore birds depart pellmell, like the disorderly land birds; the latter do not seem to care what birds lead the van or which form the rear-guard of the migrating flocks. Water birds, on the contrary, preserve the following order: one forms the apex of advance, and all the others follow successively in a double row, one to the left and one to the right. Sometimes there are more than one series than in the other, but the two rows, meeting at an angle, form a pyramidal figure...

One member of the flock usually acts as leader and, especially in the case of cranes, does this not because he alone knows the goal they seek, but that he may be on the lookout for danger, of which he warns his companions: When the leader becomes fatigued from the performance of this important work, his place in front is taken and his duties are assumed by another experienced commander.

ame le iour en vn an q̄ ... onex la mest Dieu lui comāda ꝺ ale? ꝼꝛe z
toux teꝛꝛe q̄ fuyent ꝺeꝺeꝛꝛ. z les comanꝺa q̄l ꝺeuoiēt ꝼeste z multiplieꝛ
on auteꝛ ꝺl hon ꝺe ꝺieu z off̃ce z le ꝼꝓplisme beste ꝺe touz uettes bestes. z ꝓ
ꝺontuss aꝺuiꝛēt ꝺe bestes ꝓieꝛre ꝼaffuꝛe. z ꝓuꝛ tome ilꝺ ꝼuyent ꝺieu lo ꝺona e
z ꝺi tote thoɬe en thꝛe z muɬt ꝺiꝑɬ. ꝺu tiel en le ꝼmꝺmiet en ꝼigne q̄ muɬt tiel ꝼ
ꝑluꝼes eſt̃e. tel? te ꝺeuoient ilꝺ ꝯlemenꝯneꝛ.

↩ The Rainbow

Bartholomew Anglicus (1203–1272) wrote his encyclopaedic The Properties of Things *in around 1260. In his introduction to a 1905 edition of this 'famous knowledge-book of the Middle Ages', William Morris applauded the 'quaint floweriness' of a book that was 'at once agreeable and useful'.*

Rainbow is impression gendered in an hollow cloud and dewy, disposed to rain in endless many gutters, as it were shining in a mirror, and is shapen as a bow, and sheweth divers colours, and is gendered by the beams of the sun or of the moon. And is but seldom gendered by beams of the moon, no more but twice in fifty years, as Aristotle saith.

In the rainbow, because of its clearness, be seen divers forms, kinds, and shapes that be contrary. Therefore the bow seemeth coloured, for, as Bede saith, it taketh colour of the four elements. For therein, as it were in any mirror, shineth figures and shapes and kinds of elements. For of fire he taketh red colour in the overmost part, and of earth green in the nethermost, and of the air a manner of brown colour, and of water some deal blue in the middle. And first is red colour, that cometh out of a light beam, that touches the outer part of the roundness of the cloud; then is a middle colour some deal blue, as the quality asketh, that hath mastery in the vapour, that is in the middle of the cloud. Then the nethermost seemeth a green colour in the nether part of a cloud; there the vapour is more earthly. And these colours are more principal than others. As Bede saith, and the master of stories, forty years to-fore the doom, the rainbow shall not be seen, and that shall be token of drying, and of default of elements.

❧ The Colour of the Atmosphere

Leonardo da Vinci (1452–1519) made detailed observations on the way he saw things in a series of notebooks, which are packed with ideas about painting and potential inventions (translated by Jean Paul Richter, 1888).

I say that the blueness we see in the atmosphere is not intrinsic colour, but is caused by warm vapour evaporated in minute and insensible atoms on which the solar rays fall, rendering them luminous against the infinite darkness of the fiery sphere which lies beyond and includes it. And this may be seen, as I saw it by any one going up Monte Rosa, a peak of the Alps which divide France from Italy. The base of this mountain gives birth to the four rivers which flow in four different directions through the whole of Europe. And no mountain has its base at so great a height as this, which lifts itself almost above the clouds; and snow seldom falls there, but only hail in the summer, when the clouds are highest. And this hail lies there, so that if it were not for the absorption of the rising and falling clouds, which does not happen twice in an age, an enormous mass of ice would be piled up there by the hail, and in the middle of July I found it very considerable.

There I saw above me the dark sky, and the sun as it fell on the mountain was far brighter here than in the plains below, because a smaller extent of atmosphere lay between the summit of the mountain and the sun.

Again as an illustration of the colour of the atmosphere I will mention the smoke of old and dry wood, which, as it comes out of a chimney, appears to turn very blue, when seen between the eye and the dark distance. But as it rises, and comes between the eye and the bright atmosphere, it at once shows of an ashy grey colour; and this happens because it no longer has darkness beyond it, but this bright and luminous space. If the smoke is from young, green wood, it will not appear blue, because, not being transparent and being full of superabundant moisture, it has the effect of condensed clouds which take distinct lights and shadows like a solid body. The same occurs with the atmosphere, which, when overcharged with moisture appears white, and the small amount of heated moisture makes it dark, of a dark blue colour; and this will suffice us so far as concerns the colour of the atmosphere; though it might be added that, if this transparent blue were the natural colour of the atmosphere, it would follow that wherever a larger mass of air intervened between the eye and the element of fire, the azure colour would be more intense; as we see in blue glass and in sapphires, which are darker in proportion as they are larger. But the atmosphere in such circumstances behaves in an opposite manner, inasmuch as where a greater quantity of it lies between the eye and the sphere of fire, it is seen much whiter. This occurs towards the horizon. And the less the extent of atmosphere between the eye and the sphere of fire, the deeper is the blue colour, as may be seen even on low plains.

Hence it follows, as I say, that the atmosphere assumes this azure hue by reason of the particles of moisture which catch the rays of the sun. Again, we may note the difference in particles of dust, or particles of smoke, in the sun beams admitted through holes into a dark chamber, when the former will look ash grey and the thin smoke will appear of a most beautiful blue; and it may be seen again in the dark shadows of distant mountains when the air between the eye and those shadows will look very blue, though the brightest parts of those mountains will not differ much from their true colour. But if any one wishes for a final proof let him paint a board with various colours, among them an intense black; and over all let him lay a very thin and transparent white. He will then see that this transparent white will nowhere show a more beautiful blue than over the black.

❧ Little Spirit of the Air

Richard Braithwaite (1588–1673) offered this magical characterisation of a swallow in his A Strange Metamorphosis of Man, Transformed into a Wilderness *(1634).*

The Swallow is the little spirit of the air, who will be here, and there, and everywhere, in the twinkling of an eye. He loves to dwell in the City for society's sake. His house is built in the manner of the Antipodes, in the vulgar opinion, for as their feet are opposite to ours, in consequence their houses must needs be turned upside down; and so are theirs. They have no windows, or posterns behind their houses, but all their light, egress and regress, is at the porch only, where they keep watch with their bills, both night and day, for fear of foreign invasion. Their fare is light and easy of digestion, which makes them so active and nimble as they are; not of worms, for that they hold too gross and earthly; not of corn, not to put the world to so much cost; nor of flesh, for they cannot endure the flesh pots of Egypt. They hark, hunt, and fish where they list, as being the Rangers of the Forests, allowed by nature through the privilege of their wing. He must needs fly well, that feeds on flies, who is so fleet, that he will stay by the way for no man's pleasure, for he is always set on the spur, and as it were, the Post of the Eagles' Court. The difficulty is, he can hardly stay so long in a place, as to take his message ere he goes, so tickle [light of touch] he is.

❧ A Drift of Cloud

Matsuo Bashō (1644–1694) was a Japanese poet recognised as the greatest master of the haiku form. He spent most of his life wandering in the countryside. These are the opening lines of his Narrow Road to the Deep North, *taken from Tim Chilcott's 2004 translation.*

The days and months are travellers of eternity, just like the years that come and go. For those who pass their lives afloat on boats, or face old age leading horses tight by the bridle, their journeying is life, their journeying is home. And many are the men of old who met their end upon the road.

How long ago, I wonder, did I see a drift of cloud borne away upon the wind, and ceaseless dreams of wandering become aroused? Only last year, I had been wandering along the coasts and bays; and in the autumn I swept away the cobwebs from my tumbledown hut on the banks of the Sumida and soon afterwards saw the old year out. But when the spring mists rose up into the sky, the gods of desire possessed me, and burned my mind with the longing to go beyond the barrier at Shirakawa. The spirits of the road beckoned me, and I could not concentrate on anything. So I patched up my trousers, put new cords in my straw hat, and strengthened my knees with moxa. A vision of the moon at Matsushima was already in my mind.

A haiku by Bashō:

Winter solitude
in a world of one colour
the sound of the wind.

✑ Scowling Heavens

James Thomson (1700–1748) was inspired to write pastoral poetry by an upbringing in the Cheviots, but spent most of his life in London and the south of England. Voltaire, then in exile in England, wrote that he found in him 'a great genius and a great Simplicity'.[1] He won popular acclaim with his four-part poem The Seasons, *published between 1724 and 1730. This magnificent description of the approach of a storm comes from 'Summer'.*

... A boding silence reigns,
Dread through the dun expanse; save the dull sound
That from the mountain, previous to the storm,
Rolls o'er the muttering earth, disturbs the flood,
And shakes the forest-leaf without a breath.
Prone, to the lowest vale, the aërial tribes
Descend; the tempest-loving raven scarce
Dares wing the dubious dusk. In rueful gaze
The cattle stand, and on the scowling heavens
Cast a deploring eye; by man forsook,
Who to the crowded cottage hies him fast,
Or seeks the shelter of the downward cave.
'Tis listening fear, and dumb amazement all;
When to the startled eye the sudden glance
Appears far south, eruptive through the cloud;
And following slower, in explosion vast,
The Thunder raises his tremendous voice.
At first, heard solemn o'er the verge of Heaven,
The tempest growls; but as it nearer comes,
And rolls its awful burden on the wind,
The lightnings flash a larger curve, and more
The noise astounds; till over head a sheet

---

1   *James Thomson (1700–1748): letters and documents*, ed. AD McKillop, 1958

Of livid flame discloses wide; then shuts,
And opens wider; shuts and opens still
Expansive, wrapping ether in a blaze.
Follows the loosen'd aggravated roar,
Enlarging, deepening, mingling; peal on peal
Crush'd horrible, convulsing heaven and earth.
Down comes a deluge of sonorous hail.
Or prone-descending rain. Wide-rent, the clouds
Pour a whole flood; and yet, its flame unquench'd,
The 'unconquerable lightning struggles through,
Ragged and fierce, or in red whirling balls.
And fires the mountains with redoubled rage.

✦ Poetry in Motion

Gilbert White (1720–1793) recorded these wonderful observations on the idiosyncratic flight of different birds in Selborne, on 7 August 1778.

A good ornithologist should be able to distinguish birds by their air as well as by their colours and shape, on the ground as well as on the wing, and in the bush as well as in the hand. For, though it must not be said that every species of bird has a manner peculiar to itself, yet there is somewhat in most genera at least, that at first sight discriminates them, and enables a judicious observer to pronounce upon them with some certainty. Put a bird in motion – 'Et verâ incessu patuit' [abbreviated quote from Virgil, meaning 'the goddess is revealed in her step']. Thus kites and buzzards sail round in circles with wings expanded and motionless; and it is from their gliding manner that the former are still called in the north of England gleads, from the Saxon verb glidan, to glide. The kestrel, or wind-hover, has a peculiar mode of hanging in the air in one place, his wings all the while being briskly agitated. Hen-harriers fly low over heaths or fields of corn, and beat the ground regularly like a pointer or setting-dog. Owls move in a buoyant manner, as if lighter than the air; they seem to want ballast. There is a peculiarity belonging to ravens that must draw the attention even of the most incurious; they spend all their leisure time in striking and cuffing each other on the wing in a kind of playful skirmish, and, when they move from one place to another, frequently turn on their backs with a loud croak, and seem to be falling to the ground. When this odd gesture betides them, they are scratching themselves with one foot, and thus lose the centre of gravity. Rooks sometimes dive and tumble in a frolicsome manner; crows and daws swagger in their walk; wood-peckers fly *volatu undoso*, opening and closing their wings at every stroke, and so are always rising or falling in curves. All of this genus use their tails, which incline downward, as a support while they run

up trees. Parrots, like all other hooked-clawed birds, walk awkwardly, and make use of their bill as a third foot, climbing and descending with ridiculous caution. All the gallinœ [chickens] parade and walk gracefully, and run nimbly, but fly with difficulty, with an impetuous whirring, and in a straight line. Magpies and jays flutter with powerless wings, and make no despatch; herons seem encumbered with too much sail for their light bodies, but these vast hollow wings are necessary in carrying burdens, such as large fishes and the like; pigeons, and particularly the sort called smiters, have a way of clashing their wings the one against the other over their backs with a loud snap; another variety, called tumblers, turn themselves over in the air. Some birds have movements peculiar to the season of love. Thus ringdoves, though strong and rapid at other times, yet in the spring hang about on the wing in a toying and playful manner; thus the cock-snipe while breeding, forgetting his former flight, fans the air like the windhover; and the green-finch in particular, exhibits such languishing and faltering gestures as to appear like a wounded and dying bird; the kingfisher darts along like an arrow; fern-owls, or goat-suckers, glance in the dusk over the tops of trees like a meteor; starlings, as it were, swim along, while mistle-thrushes use a wild and desultory flight; swallows sweep over the surface of the ground and water, and distinguish themselves by rapid turns and quick evolutions; swifts dash round in circles; and the bank-martin moves with frequent vacillations like a butterfly. Most of the small birds fly by jerks, rising and falling as they advance. Most small birds hop; but wagtails and larks walk moving their legs alternately. Skylarks rise and fall perpendicularly as they sing; woodlarks hang poised in the air; and titlarks rise and fall in large curves, singing in their descent. The white-throat uses odd jerks and gesticulations over the tops of hedges and bushes. All the duck-kind waddle; divers and auks walk as if fettered, and stand erect on their tails; these are the *compedes* [fetters] of Linnæus. Geese and cranes, and most wild fowls, move in figured flights, often changing their position. The secondary remiges [from the Latin oarsmen] of Tringæ, wild-ducks, and some others, are very long, and give their wings, when in motion, a hooked appearance. Dabchicks, moorhens, and coots, fly erect, with their legs hanging down, and hardly make any despatch. The reason is plain, their wings are placed too forward out of the true centre of gravity, as the legs of auks and divers are situated too backward.

❧ All the Glorious Pageantry of Heaven

Robert Blomfield (1766–1823) was a Suffolk cobbler whose poem The
Farmer's Boy *became a runaway best-seller after a local squire paid for
its publication in 1800, with illustrations by Thomas Bewick. These lines
describing the boy's duties in winter were transcribed by John Constable under
a sketch of the night sky that was inspired by them.*

GILES, ere he sleeps, his little Flock must tell.
From the fire-side with many a shrug he hies,
Glad if the full-orb'd Moon salute his eyes,
And through the unbroken stillness of the night
Shed on his path her beams of cheering light.
With saunt'ring step he climbs the distant stile,

Whilst all around him wears a placid smile;
There views the white-rob'd clouds in clusters driv'n,
And all the glorious pageantry of heav'n.
Low, on the utmost bound'ry of the sight,
The rising vapours catch the silver light;
Thence Fancy measures, as they parting fly,
Which first will throw its shadow on the eye,
Passing the source of light; and thence away,
Succeeded quick by brighter still than they.
For yet above these wafted clouds are seen
(In a remoter sky, still more serene,)
Others, detach'd in ranges through the air,
Spotless as snow, and countless as they're fair;
Scatter'd immensely wide from east to west,
The beauteous 'semblance of a Flock at rest.
These, to the raptur'd mind, aloud proclaim
Their MIGHTY SHEPHERD'S everlasting Name.

ᕃᕍ A Huge Sea of Mist

William Wordsworth (1770–1850) began to write the autobiographical poem known as The Prelude, or the Growth of a Poet's Mind *in 1798, and added to it until his death. This extract from the last book[2] describes a night-time ascent of Snowdon made in 1791.*

The Moon hung naked in a firmament
Of azure without cloud, and at my feet
Rested a silent sea of hoary mist.
A hundred hills their dusky backs upheaved
All over this still ocean; and beyond,
Far, far beyond, the solid vapours stretched,
In headlands, tongues, and promontory shapes,
Into the main Atlantic, that appeared
To dwindle, and give up his majesty,
Usurped upon far as the sight could reach.
Not so the ethereal vault; encroachment none
Was there, nor loss; only the inferior stars
Had disappeared, or shed a fainter light
In the clear presence of the full-orbed Moon,
Who, from her sovereign elevation, gazed
Upon the billowy ocean, as it lay
All meek and silent, save that through a rift–
Not distant from the shore whereon we stood,
A fixed, abysmal, gloomy, breathing-place–
Mounted the roar of waters, torrents, streams
Innumerable, roaring with one voice!
Heard over earth and sea, and, in that hour,
For so it seemed, felt by the starry heavens.

---

2   'Book 14', *The Prelude*, 1850

⚘ Sunset and Moonset

Samuel Taylor Coleridge (1772–1834) was, like his friend Wordsworth, a formidable observer of skies and atmospheric effects; these energetically written extracts are from his notebooks, which were published in 1895 as Anima Poetae.

September 14, 1801
Northern Lights remarkably fine – chiefly a purple-blue – in shooting pyramids, moved from over Bassenthwaite behind Skiddaw.

September 15, 1801
Observed the great half moon setting behind the mountain ridge, and watched the shapes its various segments presented as it slowly sunk – first the foot of a boot, all but the heel – then a little pyramid Δ – then a star of the first magnitude – indeed, it was not distinguishable from the evening star at its largest – then rapidly a smaller, a small, a very small star – and, as it diminished in size, so it grew paler in tint. And now where is it? Unseen – but a little fleecy cloud hangs above the mountain ridge, and is rich in amber light.

Bright October 21, 1803, Friday morning
A drizzling rain. Heavy masses of shapeless vapour upon the mountains (O the perpetual forms of Borrowdale!) yet it is no unbroken tale of dull sadness. Slanting pillars travel across the lake at long intervals, the vaporous mass whitens in large stains of light – on the lakeward ridge of that huge arm-chair of Lodore fell a gleam of softest light, that brought out the rich hues of the late autumn. Little woolpacks of white bright vapour rest on different summits and declivities. The vale is narrowed by the mist and cloud, yet through the wall of mist you can see into a bower of sunny light, in Borrowdale; the birds are singing in the tender rain, as if it were the rain of April, and the decaying foliage were flowers and blossoms.

The pillar of smoke from the chimney rises up in the mist, and is just distinguishable from it, and the mountain forms in the gorge of Borrowdale consubstantiate with the mist and cloud, even as the pillar'd smoke – a shade deeper and a determinate form.

Moonset, Friday, Nov. 25, 1803

After a night of storm and rain, the sky calm and white, by blue vapour thinning into formlessness instead of clouds, the mountains of height covered with snow, the secondary mountains black. The moon descending aslant the [valley], through the midst of which the great road winds, set exactly behind Whinlatter Point. She being an egg, somewhat uncouthly shaped, perhaps, but an ostrich's egg rather than any other (she is two nights more than a half-moon), she set behind the black point, fitted herself on to it like a cap of fire, then became a crescent, then a mountain of fire in the distance, then the peak itself on fire, one steady flame; then stars of the first, second and third magnitude, and vanishing, upboiled a swell of light, and in the next second the whole sky, which had been sable blue around the yellow moon, whitened and brightened for as large a space as would take the moon half an hour to descend through.

Sunset, December 6, 1803

A beautiful sunset, the sun setting behind Newlands across the foot of the lake. The sky is cloudless, save that there is a cloud on Skiddaw, one on the highest mountains in Borrowdale, some on Helvellyn, and that the sun sets in a glorious cloud. These clouds are of various shapes, various colours, and belong to their mountains and have nothing to do with the sky. N.B. – There is something metallic, silver playfully and imperfectly gilt and highly polished, or, rather, something mother-of-pearlish, in the sun-gleams on ice, thin ice.

One final gem — which I couldn't resist, having stayed for a long weekend in Coleridge's very bedroom at Greta Hall, once home to Southey and Coleridge, and now a wonderful guesthouse for Romantic enthusiasts.

Tuesday, Jan. 15, 1805

I went to the window, to empty my Urine-pot, & wondered at the simple grandeur of the View:

1. Darkness & only not utter black undistinguishableness
2. The grey-blue steely Glimmer of the Greta, & the Lake
3. The black, yet form-preserving Mountains
4. The Sky, moon-whitened there, cloud-blackened here — & yet with all its gloominess & sullenness forming a contrast with the simplicity of the Landscape beneath.

Over the black form-retaining Mountains the Horizon of Sky grey-white all round the whole Turn of my Eye the Sky above chiefly dark, but not nearly so black as the space between my eye & the Lake, which is one formless Black, or as the black nothing-but-form-&-colour Mountains beyond the grey steely glimmery Lake & River & this diminished Blackness mottled by the not-far-from-setting half-moon.

ᢒ A Sort of Tremulousness

*Swallows again, this time nesting. William's sister Dorothy Wordsworth (1771–1855) excelled at patient observations of nature. In 1802 she recorded the pertinacity of a pair of swallows who decided to build a nest above her window (*Journals of Dorothy Wordworth, *vol. 1, ed. William Knight, 1897).*

Wednesday, 16 June: The swallows come to the sitting-room window as if wishing to build, but I am afraid they will not have courage for it; but I believe they will build in my room window. They twitter, and make a bustle, and a little cheerful song, hanging against the panes of glass with their soft white bellies close to the glass and their forked fish-like tails. They swim round and round, and again they come…

Saturday, 19 June: The shutters were closed, but I heard the birds singing. There was our own thrush, shouting with an impatient

shout; so it sounded to me. The morning was still, the twittering of the little birds was very gloomy. The owls had hooted a quarter of an hour before, now the cocks were crowing, it was near daylight.

Friday, 25 June: I went, just before tea, into the garden. I looked up at my swallow's nest, and it was gone. It had fallen down. Poor little creatures, they could not themselves be more distressed than I was. I went upstairs to look at the ruins. They lay in a large heap upon the window ledge; these swallows had been ten days employed in building this nest, and it seemed to be almost finished. I had watched them early in the morning, in the day many and many a time, and in the evenings when it was almost dark. I had seen them sitting together side by side in their unfinished nest, both morning and night. When they first came about the window they used to hang against the panes, with their white bellies and their forked tails, looking like fish; but then they fluttered and sang their own little twittering song. As soon as the nest was broad enough, a sort of ledge for them, they sat both mornings and evenings, but they did not pass the night there. Watched them one morning, when William was at Eusemere, for more than an hour. Every now and then there was a motion in their wings, a sort of tremulousness, and they sang a low song to one another.

The swallows built the nest again.

Thursday, 29 June: It is now eight o'clock; I will go and see if my swallows are on their nest. Yes! there they are, side by side, both looking down into the garden. I have been out on purpose to see their faces. I knew by looking at the window that they were there...

Thursday 8 July: The swallows stole in and out of their nest, and sat there, 'whiles quite still, 'whiles they sung low for two minutes or more, at a time just like a muffled robin.

ᕍ A Brilliant Bevy

Louisa M Budgen, an American writer for children, wrote and illustrated her three-volume Episodes of Insect Life *under the pen name of Acheta* Domestica *(the Latin name for the house cricket) in 1849. A mix of poems, parables and anecdotes, it was calculated to appeal to children.*

In July 1847 we lighted on a family of little moths (large, though, as compared with leaf-miners) more profusely laden still with the seeming precious metal. We were prying, according to our wont, into one of our mines of insect treasure – the bark, namely, of a birch-tree – when we perceived on its silvery surface what seemed a little patch of veritable gold; and, in truth, a splash fresh from the crucible of the richest and the reddest could not have surpassed in hue the wings of the little moth which, till more closely scrutinized, wore its resemblance. Of these, the upper ones were almost wholly covered by burnished gilding, but slightly varie-gated with opaque white and fringed with gold. The insect being at rest, the superior pinions were alone visible, overlapping the inferior ones of dark silken grey. Having first secured, in a conven-ient pillbox, this gilded fairy, we sought where we had found her, in hopes of falling in with one or more of her bedizened fellows. Not a bit of it; but, on curiously pulling off a fragment of the birchen bark, partially detached by time or weather, we discovered, imbedded in its inner face, some dozen of small white cocoons – a few emptied of their recent occupants, of which the remainder were yet to come forth. Was it possible that our beautiful goldwing had issued from one of these silken receptacles? She certainly had, as to our infinite satisfaction was fully proved by the emergence, in a few days, of a brilliant bevy of the like lovely and splendid little creatures. Their name we cannot tell, though it may be known probably to wiser entomologists [in fact, *Tineidae* – the same family as clothes moths!].

Let us examine now a little closer into the real quality of these insect enrichments, which come certainly under the range of that comprehensive proverb, 'All is not gold that glitters.' The appearance in question is produced ... by a transparent brown varnish laid over a white substance, as in the process of gilding leather by tinfoil covered with yellow varnish, the spots of silver being simulated by the same substance covered with a skin more colourless. The silvery and golden gloss in scales of fish are accounted for in the same manner. The white liquor under them was called 'essence d'orient' by artificial pearl-makers, and they were accustomed to employ it in their manufacture.

⸎ Like a Flash of Lightning

James Audubon (1785–1861) took over a family homestead in Pennsylvania in 1803, where he developed his love of natural things, especially birds, for whom he 'felt an intimacy … bordering on frenzy'.[3] He published his five-volume Ornithological Biography *(1849) in collaboration with the Scottish naturalist William McGillivray. He took a patriotic pride in this dramatic description of the white-headed eagle, falco leucocephalus.*

The figure of this noble bird is well known throughout the civilized world, emblazoned as it is on our national standard, which waves in the breeze of every clime, bearing to distant lands the remembrance of a great people living in a state of peaceful freedom. May that peaceful freedom last for ever!

The great strength, daring, and cool courage of the White-headed Eagle, joined to his unequalled power of flight, render him highly conspicuous among his brethren. To these qualities did he add a generous disposition towards others, he might be looked up to as a model of nobility. The ferocious, overbearing, and tyrannical temper which is ever and anon displaying itself in his actions, is, nevertheless, best adapted to his state, and was wisely given him by the Creator to enable him to perform the office assigned to him.

To give you, kind reader, some idea of the nature of this bird, permit me to place you on the Mississippi, on which you may float gently along, while approaching winter brings millions of water-fowl on whistling wings, from the countries of the north, to seek a milder climate in which to sojourn for a season. The Eagle is seen perched, in an erect attitude, on the highest summit of the tallest tree by the margin of the broad stream. His glistening but stern eye looks over the vast expanse. He listens attentively to every sound that comes to his quick ear from afar, glancing now and then on

3   Richard Rhodes, *John James Audubon: The Making of an American*, 2004

the earth beneath, lest even the light tread of the fawn may pass unheard. His mate is perched on the opposite side, and should all be tranquil and silent, warns him by a cry to continue patient. At this well-known call, the male partly opens his broad wings, inclines his body a little downwards, and answers to her voice in tones not unlike the laugh of a maniac. The next moment, he resumes his erect attitude, and again all around is silent. Ducks of many species, the Teal, the Wigeon, the Mallard and others, are seen passing with great rapidity, and following the course of the current; but the Eagle heeds them not; they are at that time beneath his attention. The next moment, however, the wild trumpet-like sound of a yet distant but approaching Swan is heard. A shriek from the female Eagle comes across the stream, – for, kind reader, she is fully as alert as her mate. The latter suddenly shakes the whole of his body, and with a few touches of his bill, aided by the action of his cuticular muscles, arranges his plumage in an instant. The snow-white bird is now in sight; her long neck is stretched forward, her eye is on the watch, vigilant as that of her enemy; her large wings seem with difficulty to support the weight of her body, although they flap incessantly. So irksome do her exertions seem, that her very legs are spread beneath her tail, to aid her in her flight. She approaches, however. The Eagle has marked her for his prey. As the Swan is passing the dreaded pair, starts from his perch, in full preparation for the chase, the male bird, with an awful scream, that to the Swan's ear brings more terror than the report of the large duck-gun.

Now is the moment to witness the display of the Eagle's powers. He glides through the air like a falling star, and, like a flash of lightning, comes upon the timorous quarry, which now, in agony and despair, seeks, by various manoeuvres, to elude the grasp of his cruel talons. It mounts, doubles, and willingly would plunge into the stream, were it not prevented by the Eagle, which, long possessed of the knowledge that by such a stratagem the Swan might escape him, forces it to remain in the air by attempting to strike it with his talons from beneath. The hope of escape is soon given up by the Swan. It has already become much weakened, and its strength fails at the sight of the courage and swiftness of its antagonist. Its last gasp is about to escape, when the ferocious Eagle strikes with his talons the under side of its wing, and with unresisted power forces the bird to fall in a slanting direction upon the nearest shore.

It is then, reader, that you may see the cruel spirit of this dreaded enemy of the feathered race, whilst, exulting over his prey, he for the first time breathes at ease. He presses down his powerful feet, and drives his sharp claws deeper than ever into the heart of the dying Swan. He shrieks with delight, as he feels the last convulsions of his prey, which has now sunk under his unceasing efforts to render death as painfully felt as it can possibly be. The female has watched every movement of her mate; and if she did not assist him in capturing the Swan, it was not from want of will, but merely that she felt full assurance that the power and courage of her lord were quite sufficient for the deed. She now sails to the spot where he eagerly awaits her, and when she has arrived, they together turn the breast of the luckless Swan upwards, and gorge themselves with gore.

❧ Yellow-breeched Philosopher

Ralph Waldo Emerson (1803–1882) was a poet and essayist who championed 'the infinitude of the private man'. He valued solitude, and his writings inspired Henry David Thoreau. His poem 'The Humble-Bee' illustrates both his sense of humour and his fondness for striking metaphors. It appeared in Poems *(1847).*

Burly, dozing humble-bee,
Where thou art is clime for me.
Let them sail for Porto Rique,
Far-off heats through seas to seek;
I will follow thee alone,
Thou animated torrid-zone!
Zigzag steerer, desert cheerer,
Let me chase thy waving lines;
Keep me nearer, me thy hearer,
Singing over shrubs and vines.

Insect lover of the sun,
Joy of thy dominion!
Sailor of the atmosphere;
Swimmer through the waves of air;
Voyager of light and noon;
Epicurean of June;
Wait, I prithee, till I come
Within earshot of thy hum, –
All without is martyrdom.

When the south wind, in May days,
With a net of shining haze
Silvers the horizon wall,
And with softness touching all,

Tints the human countenance
With a colour of romance,
And infusing subtle heats,
Turns the sod to violets,
Thou, in sunny solitudes,
Rover of the underwoods,
The green silence dost displace
With thy mellow, breezy bass.

Hot midsummer's petted crone,
Sweet to me thy drowsy tone
Tells of countless sunny hours,
Long days, and solid banks of flowers;
Of gulfs of sweetness without bound
In Indian wildernesses found;
Of Syrian peace, immortal leisure,
Firmest cheer, and bird-like pleasure.

Aught unsavory or unclean
Hath my insect never seen;
But violets and bilberry bells,
Maple-sap and daffodils,
Grass with green flag half-mast high,
Succory to match the sky,
Columbine with horn of honey,
Scented fern, and agrimony,
Clover, catchfly, adder's-tongue
And brier-roses, dwelt among;
All beside was unknown waste,
All was picture as he passed.

Wiser far than human seer,
Yellow-breeched philosopher!

Seeing only what is fair,
Sipping only what is sweet,
Thou dost mock at fate and care,
Leave the chaff, and take the wheat.
When the fierce northwestern blast
Cools sea and land so far and fast,
Thou already slumberest deep;
Woe and want thou canst outsleep;
Want and woe, which torture us,
Thy sleep makes ridiculous.

ᡐ A Shroud of Dazzling Mist

Henry Alford (1810–1871) was best known as a biblical scholar, but he had a wide acquaintance among London literary figures and enjoyed travelling. In the summer of 1838, he visited the Lakes with his wife, and wrote 'Summit of Skiddaw, July 7, 1838'.

At length here stand we, wrapt as in the cloud
In which light dwelt before the sun was born,
When the great fiat issued, in the morn
Of this fair world; alone and in a shroud
Of dazzling mist, while the wind whistling loud
Buffets thy streaming locks; result forlorn
For us who up yon steep our way have worn,
Elate with hope, and of our daring proud.
Yet though no stretch of glorious prospect range
Beneath our vision, – neither Scottish coast
Nor ocean-island, nor the future boast
Of far-off hills descried, – I would not change
For aught on earth this solitary hour
Of Nature's grandest and most sacred power.

᪥ Like a Thunderbolt

Alfred, Lord Tennyson (1809–1892) journeyed across the Pyrenees with Arthur Hallam, his sister's fiancé, in 1830. He was immensely inspired by the mountains, and returned to the little Pyrenean village of Cauteretz again and again in later years. His famous poem 'The Eagle' was published in 1851.

He clasps the crag with crooked hands;
Close to the sun in lonely lands,
Ring'd with the azure world, he stands.

The wrinkled sea beneath him crawls;
He watches from his mountain walls,
And like a thunderbolt he falls.

⟪ Unspotted Whiteness

Herman Melville (1819–1891) is best known for whale lore. But his footnote to chapter 2 of Moby-Dick *(1851) is an ecstatic celebration of the albatross.*

I remember the first albatross I ever saw. It was during a prolonged gale, in waters hard upon the Antarctic seas. From my forenoon watch below, I ascended to the over-clouded deck; and there, dashed upon the main hatches, I saw a regal, feathery thing of unspotted whiteness, and with a hooked, Roman bill sublime. At intervals, it arched forth its vast archangel wings, as if to embrace some holy ark. Wondrous flutterings and throbbings shook it. Though bodily unharmed, it uttered cries, as some king's ghost in supernatural distress. Through its inexpressible, strange eyes, methought I peeped to secrets which took hold of God. As Abraham before the angels, I bowed myself; the white thing was so white, its wings so wide, and in those for ever exiled waters, I had lost the miserable warping memories of traditions and of towns. Long I gazed at that prodigy of plumage. I cannot tell, can only hint, the things that darted through me then. But at last I awoke; and turning, asked a sailor what bird was this. A goney, he replied. Goney! I never had heard that name before; is it conceivable that this glorious thing is utterly unknown to men ashore! Never! But some time after, I learned that goney was some seaman's name for albatross. So that by no possibility could Coleridge's wild Rhyme have had aught to do with those mystical impressions which were mine, when I saw that bird upon our deck. For neither had I then read the Rhyme, nor knew the bird to be an albatross. Yet, in saying this, I do but indirectly burnish a little brighter the noble merit of the poem and the poet.

I assert, then, that in the wondrous bodily whiteness of the bird chiefly lurks the secret of the spell; a truth the more evinced in this, that by a solecism of terms there are birds called grey albatrosses; and these I have frequently seen, but never with such emotions as when

I beheld the Antarctic fowl.

But how had the mystic thing been caught? Whisper it not, and I will tell; with a treacherous hook and line, as the fowl floated on the sea. At last the Captain made a postman of it; tying a lettered, leathern tally round its neck, with the ship's time and place; and then letting it escape. But I doubt not, that leathern tally, meant for man, was taken off in Heaven, when the white fowl flew to join the wing-folding, the invoking, and adoring cherubim!

ᴈ Old Ungodly Rogue

William Canton (1845–1926) grew up in Jamaica and Brittany, and was renowned as a journalist and for his stories for children. 'The Crow' appeared in A Lost Epic and Other Poems *(1887).*

With rakish eye and plenished crop,
Oblivious of the farmer's gun,
Upon the naked ash-tree top
The Crow sits basking in the sun.

An old ungodly rogue, I wot!
For, perched in black against the blue,
His feathers, torn with beak and shot,
Let woeful glints of April through.

The year's new grass, and, golden-eyed,
The daisies sparkle underneath,
And chestnut-trees on either side
Have opened every ruddy sheath.

But doubtful still of frost and snow,
The ash alone stands stark and bare,
And on its topmost twig the Crow
Takes the glad morning's sun and air.

✎ The Spirit of the Hive

Maurice Maeterlinck (1862–1949) was a Belgian Symbolist poet, playwright and novelist. He kept bees for twenty years before writing The Life of the Bee *(1901), which Edward Thomas described as 'science and poetry allied'.[4] This extract is from chapter VI, 'The Nuptial Flight'.*

They have shaken off the torpor of winter. The queen started laying again in the very first days of February, and the workers have flocked to the willows and nut-trees, gorse and violets, anemones and lung-worts. Then spring invades the earth, and cellar and stream with honey and pollen, while each day beholds the birth of thousands of bees. The overgrown males now all sally forth from their cells, and disport themselves on the combs; and so crowded does the too prosperous city become that hundreds of belated workers, coming back from the flowers towards evening, will vainly seek shelter within, and will be forced to spend the night on the threshold, where they will be decimated by the cold. Restlessness seizes the people, and the old queen begins to stir. She feels that a new destiny is being prepared. She has religiously fulfilled her duty as a good creatress; and from this duty done there result only tribulation and sorrow. An invincible power menaces her tranquillity; she will soon be forced to quit this city of hers, where she has reigned. But this city is her work, it is she, herself. She is not its queen in the sense in which men use the word. She issues no orders; she obeys, as meekly as the humblest of her subjects, the masked power, sovereignly wise, that for the present, and till we attempt to locate it, we will term the 'spirit of the hive'. But she is the unique organ of love; she is the mother of the city. She founded it amid uncertainty and poverty. She has peopled it with her own substance; and all who move within its walls – workers, males, larvae, nymphs, and the young princesses whose approaching

---

4   Edward Thomas, *Maurice Maeterlinck*, 1912

birth will hasten her own departure, one of them being already designed as her successor by the 'spirit of the hive' – all these have issued from her flanks.

What is this 'spirit of the hive' – where does it reside? It is not like the special instinct that teaches the bird to construct its well-planned nest, and then seek other skies when the day for migration returns. Nor is it a kind of mechanical habit of the race, or blind craving for life, that will fling the bees upon any wild hazard the moment an unforeseen event shall derange the accustomed order of phenomena. On the contrary, be the event never so masterful, the 'spirit of the hive' still will follow it, step by step, like an alert and quick-witted slave, who is able to derive advantage even from his master's most dangerous orders.

It disposes pitilessly of the wealth and the happiness, the liberty and life, of all this winged people; and yet with discretion, as though governed itself by some great duty. It regulates day by day the number of births, and contrives that these shall strictly accord with the number of flowers that brighten the countryside. It decrees the queen's deposition or warns her that she must depart; it compels her to bring her own rivals into the world, and rears them royally, protecting them from their mother's political hatred. So, too, in accordance with the generosity of the flowers, the age of the spring, and the probable dangers of the nuptial flight, will it permit or forbid the first-born of the virgin princesses to slay in their cradles her younger sisters, who are singing the song of the queens. At other times, when the season wanes, and flowery hours grow shorter, it will command the workers themselves to slaughter the whole impe-rial brood, that the era of revolutions may close, and work become the sole object of all. The 'spirit of the hive' is prudent and thrifty, but by no means parsimonious. And thus, aware, it would seem, that nature's laws are somewhat wild and extravagant in all that pertains to love, it tolerates, during summer days of abundance, the embar-rassing presence in the hive of three or four hundred males, from whose ranks the queen about to be born shall select her lover; three or four hundred foolish, clumsy, useless, noisy creatures, who are pretentious, gluttonous, dirty, coarse, totally and scandalously idle, insatiable, and enormous.

❧ Clear and Still

Edward Thomas (1878–1917) first made his name as a literary critic and writer of books about landscape. His essay 'Flowers of the Frost' was published in Country Life magazine, 13 February 1909. He did not try his hand at poetry until he was urged to by Robert Frost after they became friends in 1913.

Frosty nights … are often majestic, so that I wonder more people do not deliberately watch the action of the great and infinitely varied dramas of night as they watch mountains or seas. There is one such typical night, for example, which is born from a candied violet sky in the twilight without any wind. A huge edifice of sombre cloud lingers later in the south-west, crumbles gradually away and leaves a pale blue that lasts nearly till dawn. The full night is clear and still. You can count the stars, but those few are intensely bright and seem to drip with moist splendour. All is silent except for five minutes when two dog-foxes meet in a glade, and while they fight scream as wildly as cats and in similar tones, but less shrill and more malignant; the victor goes barking wearily away. Then from the north-west clouds begin to ascend, and before you are aware have covered all the sky with grey that is broken up like sun-baked mud, with watery light in the interstices; and presently the sun is seen well above the horizon, bright but with confined radiance, so that it stains only the nearest of the dark clouds, on which it rests like a gold crown, on a bier.

✍ A Trance of Flight

J A Baker (1926–1986) declared himself as obsessed by peregrine falcons as Ahab was with Moby Dick. The Peregrine (1967), which the birder Mark Cocker describes as 'still the gold standard for all nature writing', recounts a single year from October to April (probably of 1962/3) spent stalking falcons.

March 10th 1963: Towering white clouds grew in the marble sunlight of the morning. The wind eroded them to falling weirs of rain. The estuary at high tide brimmed with blue and silver light, then tarnished and thinned to grey. A falcon flew low across the marsh, weaving through the wind with sudden dips and swerves, as though moving under invisible branches and twisting between invisible trees. She flew like a big, sleepy merlin. The sun shone on the splendid burnish of her back and wings. They were a deep roan colour, the colour of a redpoll steer, like the patches of red soil that stain the ploughlands to the north. The primaries were black, with a tint of blue. The comma-shaped curl of the dark brown moustachial mark gleamed like a nostril on the white face. The hump of muscle between her wings rose and fell under the feathers as the wings moved forward and back. She looked docile, yet menacing, like a bison. Redshanks stood sleekly in the grass and watched her go by. They were quite still, save the nervous bobbing and twitching of their bright orange legs.

An hour later, from a flurry and cry of curlew, the falcon lifted clear and circled slowly up above the marsh. She glided in a thermal of warm air that bent its white bloom of cloud before the strong north wind. With rigid wings outstretched, she rose in a trance of flight, wafted upon air like a departing god. Watching the falcon receding up into the silence of the sky, I shared the exaltation and serenity of her slow ascension. As she dwindled higher, her circles were widened and stretched out by the wind, till she was only a sharp speck cutting across white cloud, a faint blur on blue sky.

She drifted idly, remote, inimical. She balanced in the wind, two thousand feet above, while the white cloud passed beyond her and went across the estuary to the south. Slowly her wings curved back. She slipped smoothly through the wind, as though she were moving forward on a wire. This mastery of the roaring wind, this majesty and noble power of flight, made me shout aloud and dance up and down with excitement. Now, I thought, I have seen the best of the peregrine; there will be no need to pursue it farther. I shall never want to search for it again. I was wrong, of course. One can never have enough.

Fire

The element of Fire is both creative and destructive, its qualities are Brightness, Thinness and Motion and its mode is Active. It is fire that we and our ancestors used to warm our homes, we use it to cook our food, we sit around it to ward off the darkness of night, and it fuels our passions.

www.thewhitegoddess.co.uk/the_elements/fire.asp

✿ An Ever-living Fire

Heraclitus (c. 540–c. 475 BC) was born at Ephesus. Only fragments remain of his notoriously obscure philosophical treatise On Nature, *which concluded that everything was and would remain in flux. Here is what he has to say about fire (translated by William Harris).*

There is exchange of all things for fire and of fire for all things, as there is of wares for gold and of gold for wares.

This universe, which is the same for all, has not been made by any god or man, but it always has been, is, and will be – an ever-living fire, kindling itself by regular measures and going out by regular measures.

The phases of fire are craving and satiety.

It throws apart and then brings together again; it advances and retires.

The transformations of fire – first, sea; and of sea, half becomes earth and half the lightning-flash.

When earth has melted into sea, the resultant amount is the same as there had been before sea became hardened into earth.

Fire lives in the death of earth, air in the death of fire, water in the death of air, and earth in the death of water.

Fire in its advance will catch all things by surprise and judge them.

✑ Huge Figures of Flame

Pliny the Younger (AD 61–c. 113) was eighteen and living with his mother at Misenum when he witnessed the eruption of Vesuvius firsthand. His uncle, the renowned naturalist, died after setting out in a small galley to rescue friends. These extracts are from letters Pliny wrote to his friend, the historian Tacitus.

Letter LXV: The cloud was rising from a mountain - at such a distance we couldn't tell which, but afterwards learned that it was Vesuvius. I can best describe its shape by likening it to a pine tree. It rose into the sky on a very long 'trunk' from which spread some 'branches.' I imagine it had been raised by a sudden blast, which then weakened, leaving the cloud unsupported so that its own weight caused it to spread sideways. Some of the cloud was white, in other parts there were dark patches of dirt and ash. … Broad sheets of flame were

lighting up many parts of Vesuvius; their light and brightness were the more vivid for the darkness of the night … The buildings were being rocked by a series of strong tremors, and appeared to have come loose from their foundations and to be sliding this way and that. Outside, however, there was danger from the rocks that were coming down, light and fire-consumed as these bits of pumice were … It was daylight now elsewhere in the world, but there the darkness was darker and thicker than any night … Then came a smell of sulphur, announcing the flames, and the flames themselves…

Letter LXVI: There had been tremors for many days previously, a common occurrence in Campania and no cause for panic. But that night the shaking grew much stronger; people thought it was an earthquake, not just a tremor … Now the day begins, with a still hesitant and almost lazy dawn. All around us buildings are shaken … In addition, it seemed as though the sea was being sucked backwards, as if it were being pushed back by the shaking of the land. Certainly the shoreline moved outwards, and many sea creatures were left on dry sand. Behind us were frightening dark clouds, rent by lightning twisted and hurled, opening to reveal huge figures of flame. These were like lightning, but bigger … Now came the dust, though still thinly. I look back: a dense cloud looms behind us, following us like a flood poured across the land. We had scarcely sat down when a darkness came that was not like a moonless or cloudy night, but more like the black of closed and unlighted rooms … It grew lighter, though that seemed not a return of day, but a sign that the fire was approaching. The fire itself actually stopped some distance away, but darkness and ashes came again, a great weight of them … At last the cloud thinned out and dwindled to no more than smoke or fog. Soon there was real daylight. The sun was even shining, though with the lurid glow it has after an eclipse. The sight that met our still terrified eyes was a changed world, buried in ash like snow.

⌖ The Burning Nest

Bartholomew Anglicus (1203–1272) described the mythical phoenix in Book 12 of his The Properties of Things, *which he wrote sometime before 1260, using many earlier writers as authorities. One of his aims was to explain scriptural allusions to natural objects: mention of the phoenix occurs in the Book of Job, who hopes to multiply his days like the phoenix. The translation here is by Robert Steele, 1893.*

Phoenix is a bird, and there is but one of that kind in all the wide world. Therefore lewd men wonder thereof, and among the Arabs, where this bird is bred, he is called singular – alone. The philosopher speaketh of this bird and saith that phoenix is a bird without mate, and liveth three hundred or five hundred years. When the which years are past, and he feeleth his own default and feebleness, he maketh a nest of right sweet-smelling sticks, that are full dry, and in summer when the western wind blows, the sticks and the nest are set on fire with burning heat of the sun, and burn strongly. Then this

bird phoenix cometh willfully into the burning nest, and is there burnt to ashes among these burning sticks, and within three days a little worm is gendered of the ashes, and waxeth little and little, and taketh feathers and is shapen and turned to a bird. Ambrose saith the same in the Hexameron: Of the humours or ashes of phoenix ariseth a new bird and waxeth, and in space of time he is clothed with feathers and wings and restored into the kind of a bird, and is the most fairest bird that is, most like to the peacock in feathers, and loveth the wilderness, and gathereth his meat of clean grains and fruits. Alan speaketh of this bird and saith, that when the highest bishop Onyas builded a temple in the city of Heliopolis in Egypt, to the likeness of the temple in Jerusalem, on the first day of Easter, when he had gathered much sweet-smelling wood, and set it on fire upon the altar to offer sacrifice, to all men's sight such a bird came suddenly, and fell into the middle of the fire, and was burnt anon to ashes in the fire of the sacrifice, and the ashes abode there, and were busily kept and saved by the commandments of the priests, and within three days, of these ashes was bred a little worm, that took the shape of a bird at the last, and flew into the wilderness.

⌁ A Shower of Fire

Robert Southey (1774–1843) was praised by the naturalist Philip Gosse for the accuracy of his description of fireflies in his epic poem Madoc *(I, v). The only time I have seen fireflies, once common in England, was in 1984, on Green Island in Poole Harbour.*

> ...Sorrowing we beheld
The night come on; but soon did night display
More wonders than it veiled: innumerous tribes
From the wood-cover swarmed, and darkness made
Their beauties visible; one while, they streamed
A bright blue radiance upon flowers that closed
Their gorgeous colours from the eye of day;
Now, motionless and dark, eluded search,
Self-shrouded; and anon, starring the sky.
Rose like a shower of fire.

❧ Phosphorescent Billows

Herman Melville (1819–1891) gave this vivid description of phosphorescent effects in his first real novel Mardi, and A Voyage Thither *(1849), which is set in the South Pacific. Nathaniel Hawthorne wrote that it had 'depths here and there that compel a man to swim for his life', but it failed to sell. This extract is from Chapter 38: The Sea On Fire*

The night ... was made memorable by a remarkable spectacle. Slumbering in the bottom of the boat, Jarl and I were suddenly awakened by Samoa. Starting, we beheld the ocean of a pallid white colour, coruscating all over with tiny golden sparkles. But the pervading hue of the water cast a cadaverous gleam upon the boat, so that we looked to each other like ghosts. For many rods astern our wake was revealed in a line of rushing illuminated foam; while here and there beneath the surface, the tracks of sharks were denoted by vivid, greenish trails, crossing and recrossing each other in every direction. Farther away, and distributed in clusters, floated on the sea, like constellations in the heavens, innumerable Medusae, a species of small, round, refulgent fish, only to be met with in the South Seas and the Indian Ocean.

Suddenly, as we gazed, there shot high into the air a bushy jet of flashes, accompanied by the unmistakable deep breathing sound of a sperm whale. Soon, the sea all round us spouted in fountains of fire; and vast forms, emitting a glare from their flanks, and ever and anon raising their heads above water, and shaking off the sparkles, showed where an immense shoal of Cachalots [sperm whales] had risen from below to sport in these phosphorescent billows.

The vapour jetted forth was far more radiant than any portion of the sea; ascribable perhaps to the originally luminous fluid contracting still more brilliancy from its passage through the spouting canal of the whales. We were in great fear, lest without any vicious intention the Leviathans might destroy us, by coming into close contact with our boat. We would have shunned them; but they were all round and round us. Nevertheless we were safe; for as we parted the pallid brine, the peculiar irradiation which shot from about our keel seemed to deter them. Apparently discovering us of a sudden, many of them plunged headlong down into the water, tossing their fiery tails high into the air, and leaving the sea still more sparkling from the violent surging of their descent.

Their general course seemed the same as our own; to the westward. To remove from them, we at last out oars, and pulled toward the north. So doing, we were steadily pursued by a solitary whale, that must have taken our *Chamois* for a kindred fish. Spite of all our efforts, he drew nearer and nearer; at length rubbing his fiery flank against the *Chamois'* gunwale, here and there leaving long strips of the glossy transparent substance which thin as gossamer invests the body of the Cachalot.

In terror at a sight so new, Samoa shrank. But Jarl and I, more used to the intimate companionship of the whales, pushed the boat away from it with our oars: a thing often done in the fishery. The close vicinity of the whale revived in the so long astute Skyeman all the enthusiasm of his daring vocation. However quiet by nature, a thorough-bred whaleman betrays no little excitement in sight of his game. And it required some persuasion to prevent Jarl from darting his harpoon: insanity under present circumstances; and of course without object. But 'Oh! for a dart,' cried my Viking. And 'Where's now our old ship?' he added reminiscently.

But to my great joy the monster at last departed; rejoining the shoal, whose lofty spoutings of flame were still visible upon the distant line of the horizon; showing there, like the fitful starts of the Aurora Borealis. The sea retained its luminosity for about three hours; at the expiration of half that period beginning to fade; and excepting occasional faint illuminations consequent upon the rapid darting of fish under water, the phenomenon at last wholly disappeared.

⚘ The Bottomless Pit

The intrepid traveller Isabella Bird (1831–1904) visited Hawaii in 1872. Her bold descent into the crate of a volcano is described in The Hawaiian Archipelago *(1875).*

The first descent down the terminal wall of the crater is very precipitous, but it and the slope which extends to the second descent are thickly covered with ohias, ohelos (a species of whortleberry), sadlerias, polypodiums, silver grass, and a great variety of bulbous plants many of which bore clusters of berries of a brilliant turquoise blue. The 'beyond' looked terrible. I could not help clinging to these vestiges of the kindlier mood of nature in which she sought to cover the horrors she had wrought. The next descent is over rough blocks and ridges of broken lava, and appears to form part of a break which extends irregularly round the whole crater, and which probably marks a tremendous subsidence of its floor. Here the last apparent vegetation was left behind, and the familiar earth. We were in a new Plutonic region of blackness and awful desolation, the accustomed sights and sounds of nature all gone. Terraces, cliffs, lakes, ridges, rivers, mountain sides, whirlpools, chasms of lava surrounded us, solid, black, and shining, as if vitrified, or an ashen grey, stained yellow with sulphur here and there, or white with alum. The lava was fissured and upheaved everywhere by earthquakes, hot underneath, and emitting a hot breath.

After more than an hour of very difficult climbing we reached the lowest level of the crater, pretty nearly a mile across, presenting from above the appearance of a sea at rest, but on crossing it we found it to be an expanse of waves and convolutions of ashy-coloured lava, with huge cracks filled up with black iridescent rolls of lava, only a few weeks old. Parts of it are very rough and ridgy, jammed together like field ice, or compacted by rolls of lava which may have swelled up from beneath, but the largest part of the area presents the appearance of huge coiled hawsers, the ropy formation of the lava rendering the illusion almost perfect. These are riven by deep cracks which emit hot sulphurous vapours. Strange to say, in one of these, deep down in that black and awful region, three slender metamorphosed ferns were growing, three exquisite forms, the fragile heralds of the great forest of vegetation, which probably in coming years will clothe this pit with beauty. Truly they seemed to speak of the love of God. On our right there was a precipitous ledge, and a recent flow of lava had poured over it, cooling as it fell into columnar shapes as symmetrical as those of Staffa. It took us a full hour to cross this deep depression, and as long to master a steep hot ascent of about 400 feet, formed by a recent lava-flow from Hale-mau-mau into the basin. This lava hill is an extraordinary sight—a flood of molten stone, solidifying as it ran down the declivity, forming arrested waves, streams, eddies, gigantic convolutions, forms of snakes, stems of trees, gnarled roots, crooked water-pipes, all involved and contorted on a gigantic scale, a wilderness of force and dread. Over one steeper place the lava had run in a fiery cascade about 100 feet wide. Some had reached the ground, some had been arrested midway, but all had taken the aspect of stems of trees. In some of the crevices I picked up a quantity of very curious filamentose lava, known as 'Pele's hair.' It resembles coarse spun glass, and is of a greenish or yellowish-brown colour. In many places the whole surface of the lava is covered with this substance seen through a glazed medium. During eruptions, when fire-fountains play to a great height, and drops of lava are thrown in all directions, the wind spins them out in clear green or yellow threads two or three feet long, which catch and adhere to projecting points.

As we ascended, the flow became hotter under our feet, as well as more porous and glistening. It was so hot that a shower of rain hissed as it fell upon it. The crust became increasingly insecure, and necessitated our walking in single file with the guide in front, to test the security of the footing. I fell through several times, and always into holes full of sulphurous steam, so malignantly acid that my strong dog-skin gloves were burned through as I raised myself on my hands.

We had followed a lava-flow for thirty miles up to the crater's brink, and now we had toiled over recent lava for three hours, and by all calculation were close to the pit, yet there was no smoke or sign of fire, and I felt sure that the volcano had died out for once for our especial disappointment. Indeed, I had been making up my mind for disappointment since we left the crater-house, in consequence of reading seven different accounts, in which language was exhausted in describing Kilauea.

Suddenly, just above, and in front of us, gory drops were tossed in air, and springing forwards we stood on the brink of Hale-mau-mau, which was about 35 feet below us. I think we all screamed, I know we all wept, but we were speechless, for a new glory and terror had been added to the earth. It is the most unutterable of wonderful things. The words of common speech are quite useless. It is unimaginable, indescribable, a sight to remember for ever, a sight which at once took possession of every faculty of sense and soul, removing one altogether out of the range of ordinary life. Here was the real 'bottomless pit'—the 'fire which is not quenched'—'the place of hell'—'the lake which burneth with fire and brimstone'—the 'everlasting burnings'—the fiery sea whose waves are never weary. There were groanings, rumblings, and detonations, rushings, hissings, and splashings, and the crashing sound of breakers on the coast, but it was the surging of fiery waves upon a fiery shore.

ॐ Blown to Bits

R M Ballantyne (1825–1894) never visited the China Seas, and his vivid description of the 1883 eruption of Krakatoa that is central to Blown to Bits, or The Lonely Man of Rakala *(1889) was derived from the official report of the eruption by the Krakatoa committee; he also acknowledges Alfred Wallace's* The Malay Archipelago *(1869).*

The water had assumed an appearance of inky blackness, and large masses of pumice were floating past, among which were numerous dead bodies of men, women, and children, intermingled with riven trees, fences, and other wreckage from the land, showing that the two great waves which had already passed under the vessel had caused terrible devastation on some parts of the shore. To add to the horror of the scene large sea-snakes were seen swimming wildly about, as if seeking to escape from the novel dangers that surrounded them. The sailors looked on in awe-stricken silence…

A few minutes later there came a crash, followed by a spout of smoke, fire, steam, and molten lava, compared to which all that had gone before seemed insignificant! The crash was indescribable! As we have said elsewhere, the sound of it was heard many hundreds of miles from the seat of the volcano, and its effects were seen and felt right round the world.

The numerous vents which had previously been noticed on Krakatoa must at that moment have been blown into one, and the original crater of the old volcano—said to have been about six miles in diameter—must have resumed its destructive work. All the eye-witnesses who were near the spot at the time, and sufficiently calm to take note of the terrific events of that morning, are agreed as to the splendour of the electrical phenomena displayed during this paroxysmal outburst. One who, at the time, was forty miles distant speaks of the great vapour-cloud looking 'like an immense wall or blood-red curtain with edges of all shades of yellow, and bursts of

forked lightning at times rushing like large serpents through the air'. Another says that 'Krakatoa appeared to be alight with flickering flames rising behind a dense black cloud'. A third recorded that 'the lightning struck the mainmast conductor five or six times', and that 'the mud-rain which covered the decks was phosphorescent, while the rigging presented the appearance of St. Elmo's fire'.

It may be remarked here, in passing, that giant steam-jets rushing through the orifices of the earth's crust constitute an enormous hydro-electric engine; and the friction of ejected materials striking against each other in ascending and descending also generates electricity, which accounts to some extent for the electrical condition of the atmosphere.

In these final and stupendous outbursts the volcano was expending its remaining force in breaking up and ejecting the solid lava which constituted its framework, and not in merely vomiting forth the lava-froth, or pumice, which had characterised the earlier stages of the eruption. In point of fact – as was afterwards clearly ascertained by careful soundings and estimates, taking the average height of the missing portion at 700 feet above water, and the depth at 300 feet below it – two-thirds of the island were blown entirely off the face of the earth. The mass had covered an area of nearly six miles, and is estimated as being equal to 1 cubic miles of solid matter which, as Moses expressed it, was blown to bits!

If this had been all, it would have been enough to claim the attention and excite the wonder of the intelligent world—but this was not nearly all, as we shall see, for saddest of all the incidents connected with the eruption is the fact that upwards of thirty-six thousand human beings lost their lives.

◌❧ Promethean Rebellion

Thomas Hardy (1840–1928) conjured up the ancient magic of bonfires in his
Return of the Native *(1878).*

It seemed as if the bonfire-makers were standing in some radiant upper storey of the world, detached from and independent of the dark stretches below. The heath down there was now a vast abyss, and no longer a continuation of what they stood on; for their eyes, adapted to the blaze, could see nothing of the deeps beyond its influence. Occasionally, it is true, a more vigorous flare than usual from their faggots sent darting lights like aides-de-camp down the inclines to some distant bush, pool, or patch of white sand, kindling these to replies of the same colour, till all was lost in darkness again. Then the whole black phenomenon beneath represented Limbo as viewed from the brink by the sublime Florentine in his vision, and the muttered articulations of the wind in the hollows were as complaints and petitions from the 'souls of mighty worth' suspended therein.

It was as if these men and boys had suddenly dived into past ages, and fetched therefrom an hour and deed which had before been familiar with this spot. The ashes of the original British pyre which blazed from that summit lay fresh and undisturbed in the barrow beneath their tread. The flames from funeral piles long ago kindled there had shone down upon the lowlands as these were shining now. Festival fires to Thor and Woden had followed on the same ground and duly had their day. Indeed, it is pretty well known that such blazes as this the heathmen were now enjoying are rather the lineal descendants from jumbled Druidical rites and Saxon ceremonies than the invention of popular feeling about Gunpowder Plot.

Moreover to light a fire is the instinctive and resistant act of man when, at the winter ingress, the curfew is sounded throughout Nature. It indicates a spontaneous, Promethean rebelliousness against that fiat that this recurrent season shall bring foul times, cold darkness, misery and death. Black chaos comes, and the fettered gods of the earth say, Let there be light.

The brilliant lights and sooty shades which struggled upon the skin and clothes of the persons standing round caused their linea- ments and general contours to be drawn with Dureresque vigour and dash. Yet the permanent moral expression of each face it was impossible to discover, for as the nimble flames towered, nodded, and swooped through the surrounding air, the blots of shade and flakes of light upon the countenances of the group changed shape and position endlessly. All was unstable; quivering as leaves, evanescent as lightning. Shadowy eye-sockets, deep as those of a death's head, suddenly turned into pits of lustre: a lantern-jaw was cavernous, then it was shining; wrinkles were emphasized to ravines, or obliterated entirely by a changed ray. Nostrils were dark wells; sinews in old necks were gilt mouldings; things with no particular polish on them were glazed; bright objects, such as the tip of a furze-hook one of the men carried, were as glass; eyeballs glowed like little lanterns. Those whom Nature had depicted as merely quaint became grotesque, the grotesque became preternatural; for all was in extremity.

✒ Blood-red Orange

Robert Louis Stevenson (1850–1894) had an eye for detail and the knack of vividly conjuring up natural phenomena. 'Winter-time' is from A Child's Garden of Verses *(1885).*

Late lies the wintry sun a-bed,
A frosty, fiery sleepy-head;
Blinks but an hour or two; and then,
A blood-red orange, sets again.

Before the stars have left the skies,
At morning in the dark I rise;
And shivering in my nakedness,
By the cold candle, bathe and dress.

Close by the jolly fire I sit
To warm my frozen bones a bit;
Or with a reindeer-sled, explore
The colder countries round the door.

When to go out, my nurse doth wrap
Me in my comforter and cap;
The cold wind burns my face, and blows
Its frosty pepper up my nose.

Black are my steps on silver sod;
Thick blows my frosty breath abroad;
And tree and house, and hill and lake,
Are frosted like a wedding-cake.

ᴥ Wild Fingers of Fire

Lawrence Binyon (1869–1943) was born in Yorkshire, and spent much of his life working in the British Museum's Department of Prints and Drawings. He retired in 1933 to Streatley, where he continued to write poetry. 'The Burning of the Leaves' is the title poem of his 1944 collection.

Now is the time for the burning of the leaves.
They go to the fire; the nostril pricks with smoke
Wandering slowly into a weeping mist.
Brittle and blotched, ragged and rotten sheaves!
A flame seizes the smouldering ruin and bites
On stubborn stalks that crackle as they resist.

The last hollyhock's fallen tower is dust;
All the spices of June are a bitter reek,
All the extravagant riches spent and mean.
All burns! The reddest rose is a ghost;
Sparks whirl up, to expire in the mist: the wild
Fingers of fire are making corruption clean.

Now is the time for stripping the spirit bare,
Time for the burning of days ended and done,
Idle solace of things that have gone before:
Rootless hope and fruitless desire are there;
Let them go to the fire, with never a look behind.
The world that was ours is a world that is ours no more.

They will come again, the leaf and the flower, to arise
From squalor of rottenness into the old splendour,
And magical scents to a wondering memory bring;
The same glory, to shine upon different eyes.
Earth cares for her own ruins, naught for ours.
Nothing is certain, only the certain spring.

᪾ Lightning Javelins

Robert Service (1874–1958), the Preston-born 'Bard of the Yukon', is most renowned for doggerel ballads like 'The Shooting of Dan McGrew', but his years in the Canadian wilderness made him an acute observer of natural things. The extracts below are from 'Ballad of the Northern Lights', which appeared in Ballads of a Cheechako *(1909).*

The short-lived sun had a leaden glare and the darkness came too
   soon,
And stationed there with a solemn stare was the pinched, anaemic
   moon...
Oh, it was wild and weird and wan, and ever in camp o' nights
We would watch and watch the silver dance of the mystic
   Northern Lights.
And soft they danced from the Polar sky and swept in primrose haze;
And swift they pranced with their silver feet, and pierced with a
   blinding blaze.
They danced a cotillion in the sky; they were rose and silver shod;
It was not good for the eyes of man – 'twas a sight for the eyes of
   God.
It made us mad and strange and sad, and the gold whereof we
   dreamed
Was all forgot, and our only thought was of the lights that gleamed.

Oh, the tundra sponge it was golden brown, and some was a bright
   blood-red;
And the reindeer moss gleamed here and there like the tombstones
   of the dead.
And in and out and around about the little trail ran clear,
And we hated it with a deadly hate and we feared with a deadly fear.
And the skies of night were alive with light, with a throbbing,
   thrilling flame;

Amber and rose and violet, opal and gold it came.
It swept the sky like a giant scythe, it quivered back to a wedge;
Argently bright, it cleft the night with a wavy golden edge.
Pennants of silver waved and streamed, lazy banners unfurled;
Sudden splendours of sabres gleamed, lightning javelins were
   hurled.
There in our awe we crouched and saw with our wild, uplifted eyes
Charge and retire the hosts of fire in the battlefield of the skies.
But all things come to an end at last, and the muskeg melted away,
And frowning down to bar our path a muddle of mountains lay...

And on we went on our woeful way, wrapped in a daze of dream,

And the Northern Lights in the crystal nights came forth with a
mystic gleam.
They danced and they danced the devil-dance over the naked snow;
And soft they rolled like a tide upshoaled with a ceaseless ebb and
flow.
They rippled green with a wondrous sheen, they fluttered out like
a fan;
They spread with a blaze of rose-pink rays never yet seen of man.
They writhed like a brood of angry snakes, hissing and sulphur pale;
Then swift they changed to a dragon vast, lashing a cloven tail.
It seemed to us, as we gazed aloft with an everlasting stare,
The sky was a pit of bale and dread, and a monster revelled there...

We climbed the rise of a hog-back range that was desolate and drear,
Day after day was dark as death, but ever and ever at nights,
With a brilliancy that grew and grew, blazed up the Northern
Lights.
They rolled around with a soundless sound like softly bruiséd silk;
They poured into the bowl of the sky with the gentle flow of milk.
In eager, pulsing violet their wheeling chariots came,
Or they poised above the Polar rim like a coronal of flame.
From depths of darkness fathomless their lancing rays were hurled,
Like the all-combining searchlights of the navies of the world.
There on the roof-pole of the world as one bewitched I gazed,
And howled and grovelled like a beast as the awful splendours
blazed.

ᕬ Green Fires

D H Lawrence (1889–1930) was living in Cornwall when he wrote 'The Enkindled Spring', which appears in Amores *(1916). Although its fires are metaphorical rather than real, the imagery is irresistible.*

This spring as it comes bursts up in bonfires green,
Wild puffing of emerald trees, and flame-filled bushes,
Thorn-blossom lifting in wreaths of smoke between
Where the wood fumes up and the watery, flickering rushes.

I am amazed at this spring, this conflagration
Of green fires lit on the soil of the earth, this blaze
Of growing, and sparks that puff in wild gyration,
Faces of people streaming across my gaze.

And I, what fountain of fire am I among
This leaping combustion of spring? My spirit is tossed
About like a shadow buffeted in the throng
Of flames, a shadow that's gone astray, and is lost.

✸ Burning Juniper

Edward Abbey (1927–1987) was an environmental campaigner with radical views. He was born in Indiana, and fell in love with the desert during a hitch-hiking trip in 1946. From 1956–57, he worked as a ranger in The Arches National Park. This extract is from Desert Solitaire: A Season in the Wilderness *(1966), which celebrated his time there.*

I range around the trailer, pick up some dead sticks from under the junipers, and build a squaw fire for company.

Dark clouds sailing overhead across the fields of the stars. Stars which are unusually bold and close, with an icy glitter in their light – glints of blue, emerald, gold…

A yellow planet floats on the west, brightest object in the sky. Venus. I listen closely for the call of an owl, a dove, a nighthawk. But can hear only the crackle of my fire, a breath of wind.

The fire. The odour of burning juniper is the sweetest fragrance on the face of the earth, in my honest judgment; I doubt if all the smoking censers of Dante's paradise could equal it. One breath of juniper smoke, like the perfume of sagebrush after rain, evokes in magical catalysis, like certain music, the space and light and clarity and piercing strangeness of the American West. Long may it burn.

The little fire wavers, flickers, begins to die. I break another branch of juniper over my knee and add the fragments to the heap of coals. A wisp of bluish smoke goes up, and the wood, arid as the rock from which it came, blossoms out in fire…

I wait and watch, guarding the desert, the sand and barren rock, the isolated junipers and scattered clumps of sage surrounding me in stillness and simplicity under the starlight.

❧ Fit for a Queen

The burning properties of wood are much debated in my family: I favour sweet-smelling fruitwood for the open fire, well-aged beech and ash in the wood-burning stove, squeezed orange or lemon husks and fir cones dried in the oven for kindling. This is our favourite among the many advice rhymes on the subject.

Beechwood fires burn bright and clear
If the logs are kept a year
Store your beech for Christmastide
With new holly laid beside
Chestnuts only good they say
If for years 'tis stacked away
Birch and firwood burn too fast
Blaze too bright and do not last
Flames from larch will shoot up high
Dangerously the sparks will fly
But Ashwood green and Ashwood brown
Are fit for a Queen with a golden crown

Oaken logs, if dry and old
Keep away the winters cold
Poplar gives a bitter smoke
Fills your eyes and makes you choke
Elmwood burns like churchyard mould
Even the very flames burn cold
Hawthorn bakes the sweetest bread
So it is in Ireland said
Applewood will scent the room
Pear's wood smells like a flower in bloom
But Ashwood wet and Ashwood dry
A King may warm his slippers by.

Water

Water does not resist. Water flows. When you plunge your hand into it, all you feel is a caress. Water is not a solid wall, it will not stop you. But water always goes where it wants to go, and nothing in the end can stand against it.

Margaret Atwood, *The Penelopiad*, 2005

✒ Bending Like a Bow

Michael Drayton (1563–1631) described the characteristics of British rivers in his Poly-olbion *(1612): he was also an observant naturalist. Here he describes the salmon leap on the Tivy [Teifi], which runs through Cardigan and Newcastle Emlyn in Wales.*

Now Tivy, let us tell thy sundry glories here.
When as the salmon seeks a fresher stream to find
(Which hither from the sea comes yearly by his kind,
As he in season grows) and stems the wat'ry tract
Where Tivy, falling down, doth make a cataract,
Forc'd by the rising rocks that there her course oppose,
As though within their bounds they meant her to inclose;
Here, when the labouring fish doth at the foot arrive,
And finds that by his strength but vainly he doth strive,
His tail takes in his teeth, and bending like a bow,
That's to the compass drawn, aloft himself doth throw:
Then springing at his height, as doth a little wand,
That bended end to end, and flerted from the hand,
Far off itself doth cast ; so doth the salmon vault.
And if at first he fail, his second summersaut
He instantly assays; and from his nimble ring,
Still yarking, never leaves, until himself he fling
Above the streamful top of the surrounded heap.

❧ Nurs'd in Ocean's Pearly Caves

Erasmus Darwin (1731–1802), grandfather of the more famous Charles, was himself a naturalist of note. His 'Emigration of the Animals from the Sea' is from Canto V of his Temple of Nature *(1803).*

Organic Life beneath the shoreless waves
Was born and nurs'd in Ocean's pearly caves;
First forms minute, unseen by spheric glass,
Move on the mud, or pierce the watery mass;
These, as successive generations bloom,
New powers acquire, and larger limbs assume;
Whence countless groups of vegetation spring,
And breathing realms of fin, and feet, and wing…

Now in vast shoals beneath the brineless tide,
On earth's firm crust testaceous tribes reside;
Age after age expands the peopled plain,
The tenants perish, but their cells remain;
Whence coral walls and sparry hills ascend
From pole to pole, and round the line extend.

Next when imprison'd fires in central caves
Burst the firm earth, and drank the headlong waves;
And, as new airs with dread explosion swell,
Form'd lava-isles, and continents of shell;
Pil'd rocks on rocks, on mountains mountains raised,
And high in heaven the first volcanoes blazed;
In countless swarms an insect-myriad moves
From sea-fan gardens, and from coral groves;
Leaves the cold caverns of the deep, and creeps
On shelving shores, or climbs on rocky steeps.
As in dry air the sea-born stranger roves,

Each muscle quickens, and each sense improves;
Cold gills aquatic form respiring lungs,
And sounds aerial flow from slimy tongues.

So Trapa rooted in pellucid tides,
In countless threads her breathing leaves divides,
Waves her bright tresses in the watery mass,
And drinks with gelid gills the vital gas;
Then broader leaves in shadowy files advance,
Spread o'er the crystal flood their green expanse;
And, as in air the adherent dew exhales,
Courth the warm sun, and breathe ethereal gales.

So still the Tadpole cleaves the watery vale
With balanc'd fins, and undulating tail;
New lungs and limbs proclaim his second birth,
Breath the dry air, and bound upon the earth.
So from deep lakes the dread Musquito springs,

DOLPHIN

CACHALOT or SPERMACETI WHALE

Drinks the soft breeze, and dries his tender wings,
In twinkling squadrons cuts his airy way,
Dips his red trunk in blood, and man his prey.

So still the Diodons, amphibious tribe,
With two-fold lungs the sea or air imbibe;
Allied to fish, the lizard cleaves the flood
With one-cell'd heart, and dark frigescent blood;
Half-reasoning Beavers long-unbreathing dart
Through Erie's waves with perforated heart;
With gills and lungs respiring Lampreys steer,
Kiss the rude rocks, and suck till they adhere;
The lazy Remora's inhaling lips,
Hung on the keel, retard the struggling ships;
With gills pulmonic breathes the enormous Whale,
And spouts aquatic columns to the gale;
Sports on the shining wave at noontide hours,
And shifting rainbows crest the rising showers.

◌Გ The Ocean's Produce

George Crabbe (1754–1832) was called by Lord Byron 'nature's sternest painter, yet the best'. This ramble along the seashore is from The Borough *(1810), a long descriptive poem set in his native Aldeburgh. It featured Peter Grimes, and inspired an opera by Benjamin Britten.*

That winding streamlet, limpid, lingering slow,
Where the reeds whisper when the zephyrs blow;
Where in the midst, upon a throne of green,
Sits the large Lily as the water's queen;
And makes the current, forced awhile to stay,
Murmur and bubble as it shoots away;
Draw then the strongest contrast to that stream,
And our broad river will before thee seem.

With ceaseless motion comes and goes the tide,
Flowing, it fills the channel vast and wide;
Then back to sea, with strong majestic sweep
It rolls, in ebb yet terrible and deep;
Here Samphire-banks and Saltwort bound the flood,
There stakes and sea-weeds withering on the mud;
And higher up, a ridge of all things base,
Which some strong tide has roll'd upon the place...

Now is it pleasant in the Summer-eve,
When a broad shore retiring waters leave,
Awhile to wait upon the firm fair sand,
When all is calm at sea, all still at land;
And there the ocean's produce to explore,
As floating by, or rolling on the shore:
Those living jellies which the flesh inflame,
Fierce as a nettle, and from that its name;

Some in huge masses, some that you may bring
In the small compass of a lady's ring;
Figured by hand divine – there's not a gem
Wrought by man's art to be compared to them;
Soft, brilliant, tender, through the wave they glow,
And make the moonbeam brighter where they flow.
Involved in sea-wrack, here you find a race
Which science, doubting, knows not where to place;
On shell or stone is dropp'd the embryo-seed,
And quickly vegetates a vital breed.
While thus with pleasing wonder you inspect
Treasures the vulgar in their scorn reject,
See as they float along th' entangled weeds
Slowly approach, upborne on bladdery beads;
Wait till they land, and you shall then behold
The fiery sparks those tangled fronds infold,
Myriads of living points; th' unaided eye
Can but the fire and not the form descry.
And now your view upon the ocean turn,
And there the splendour of the waves discern;
Cast but a stone, or strike them with an oar,
And you shall flames within the deep explore;
Or scoop the stream phosphoric as you stand,
And the cold flames shall flash along your hand;
When, lost in wonder, you shall walk and gaze
On weeds that sparkle, and on waves that blaze.

☙ The Old Magnificent Species

William Wordsworth (1770–1850) offered this lovely description of swans in
An Epistle in Verse, Addressed to a Young Lady *(1793). 'The young Lady to*
whom this was addressed was my Sister', Wordsworth explains in a preface to
the poem. 'There were two pairs of [swans] that divided the lake of Esthwaite
and its in-and-out-flowing streams between them, never trespassing a single
yard upon each other's separate domain. They were of the old magnificent species,
bearing in beauty and majesty about the same relation to the Thames swan
which that does to the goose.'

'Tis pleasant near the tranquil lake to stray
Where, winding on along some secret bay,
The swan uplifts his chest, and backward flings
His neck, a varying arch, between his towering wings:
The eye that marks the gliding creature sees
How graceful, pride can be, and how majestic, ease,
While tender cares and mild domestic loves
With furtive watch pursue her as she moves,
The female with a meeker charm succeeds,
And her brown little-ones around her leads,
Nibbling the water lilies as they pass,
Or playing wanton with the floating grass.
She, in a mother's care, her beauty's pride
Forgetting, calls the wearied to her side;
Alternately they mount her back, and rest
Close by her mantling wings' embraces prest.
Long may they float upon this flood serene;
Theirs be these holms untrodden, still, and green,
Where leafy shades fence off the blustering gale,
And breathes in peace the lily of the vale!
Yon isle ... conceals their home, their hut-like bower;
Green water-rushes overspread the floor;

Long grass and willows form the woven wall,
And swings above the roof the poplar tall.
Thence issuing often with unwieldy stalk,
They crush with broad black feet their flowery walk;
Or, from the neighbouring water, hear at morn
The hound, the horse's tread, and mellow horn;
Involve their serpent-necks in changeful rings,
Rolled wantonly between their slippery wings,
Or, starting up with noise and rude delight,
Force half upon the wave their cumbrous flight.

᎒ᕱ Spouting and Frisking

Robert Southey (1774–1843), then Poet Laureate, wrote the delightful onomatopoeic 'Cataract at Lodore' in 1820 to amuse and educate his children, whom he was bringing up at Greta Hall, near Grasmere. The poem resembles a waterfall, widening as it runs down the page. The famous 'cataract' is on the Watendlath Beck, which runs into the southern end of Derwentwater at Lodore.

'How does the water
 Come down at Lodore?'
 My little boy asked me
 Thus, once on a time;
 And moreover he tasked me
 To tell him in rhyme.
 Anon, at the word,
 There first came one daughter,
 And then came another,
 To second and third
 The request of their brother,
 And to hear how the water
 Comes down at Lodore,
 With its rush and its roar,
 As many a time
 They had seen it before.
 So I told them in rhyme,
 For of rhymes I had store;
 And 'twas in my vocation
 For their recreation
 That so I should sing;
 Because I was Laureate
 To them and the King.

From its sources which well
In the tarn on the fell;
From its fountains
In the mountains,
Its rills and its gills;
Through moss and through brake,
It runs and it creeps
For a while, till it sleeps
In its own little lake.
And thence at departing,
Awakening and starting,
It runs through the reeds,
And away it proceeds,
Through meadow and glade,
In sun and in shade,
And through the wood-shelter,
Among crags in its flurry,
Helter-skelter,
Hurry-skurry.
Here it comes sparkling,
And there it lies darkling;
Now smoking and frothing
Its tumult and wrath in,
Till, in this rapid race
On which it is bent,
It reaches the place
Of its steep descent.

The cataract strong
Then plunges along,
Striking and raging

As if a war raging
Its caverns and rocks among;
Rising and leaping,
Sinking and creeping,
Swelling and sweeping,
Showering and springing,
Flying and flinging,
Writhing and ringing,
Eddying and whisking,
Spouting and frisking,
Turning and twisting,
Around and around
With endless rebound:
Smiting and fighting,
A sight to delight in;
Confounding, astounding,
Dizzying and deafening the ear with its sound.

Collecting, projecting,
Receding and speeding,
And shocking and rocking,
And darting and parting,
And threading and spreading,
And whizzing and hissing,
And dripping and skipping,
And hitting and splitting,
And shining and twining,
And rattling and battling,
And shaking and quaking,
And pouring and roaring,
And waving and raving,
And tossing and crossing,
And flowing and going,

And running and stunning,
And foaming and roaming,
And dinning and spinning,
And dropping and hopping,
And working and jerking,
And guggling and struggling,
And heaving and cleaving,
And moaning and groaning;

And glittering and frittering,
And gathering and feathering,

And whitening and brightening,
And quivering and shivering,
And hurrying and skurrying,
And thundering and floundering;

Dividing and gliding and sliding,
And falling and brawling and sprawling,
And driving and riving and striving,
And sprinkling and twinkling and wrinkling,
And sounding and bounding and rounding,
And bubbling and troubling and doubling,
And grumbling and rumbling and tumbling,
And clattering and battering and shattering;

Retreating and beating and meeting and sheeting,
Delaying and straying and playing and spraying,
Advancing and prancing and glancing and dancing,
Recoiling, turmoiling and toiling and boiling,
And gleaming and streaming and steaming and beaming,
And rushing and flushing and brushing and gushing,
And flapping and rapping and clapping and slapping,
And curling and whirling and purling and twirling,
And thumping and plumping and bumping and jumping,
And dashing and flashing and splashing and clashing;
And so never ending, but always descending,
Sounds and motions for ever and ever are blending
All at once and all o'er, with a mighty uproar, -
And this way the water comes down at Lodore.

❧ The Image of Eternity

George Gordon, Lord Byron (1788–1824) claims that he 'woke up one morning and found myself famous' after the publication of the first two cantos of Childe Harold's Pilgrimage *(1812). It was the fruit of his travels in Portugal, the Levant and Italy. These extracts describing the sea are from the third canto (stanzas 183–184).*

Thou glorious mirror, where the Almighty's form
Glasses itself in tempests; in all time,
Calm or convulsed – in breeze, or gale, or storm,
Icing the pole, or in the torrid clime
Dark-heaving; – boundless, endless, and sublime –
The image of Eternity – the throne
Of the Invisible; even from out thy slime
The monsters of the deep are made; each zone
Obeys thee: thou goest forth, dread, fathomless, alone.

And I have loved thee, Ocean! and my joy
Of youthful sports was on thy breast to be
Borne like thy bubbles, onward: from a boy
I wantoned with thy breakers – they to me
Were a delight; and if the freshening sea
Made them a terror – 'twas a pleasing fear,
For I was as it were a child of thee,
And trusted to thy billows far and near,
And laid my hand upon thy mane – as I do here.

❧ River Scene

John Clare (1793–1864), a self-taught poet who grew up in Northamptonshire, is perhaps the greatest of English nature-writers. This is my first mention of him only because he is so much anthologised. In 'The Fens', written between 1824 and 1836, he describes the flat fenlands near his birthplace with exact observation and affectionate humour, ending in regret that they are being drained for crops.[5]

…There's not a hill in all the view,
Save that a forked cloud or two
Upon the verge of distance lies
And into mountains cheats the eyes.
And as to trees the willows wear
Lopped heads as high as bushes are;
Some taller things the distance shrouds
That may be trees or stacks or clouds
Or may be nothing; still they wear
A semblance where there's nought to spare.
Among the tawny tasselled reed
The ducks and ducklings float and feed.
With head oft dabbing in the flood
They fish all day the weedy mud,
And tumbler-like are bobbing there,
Heels topsy turvy in the air.
The geese in troops come droving up,
Nibble the weeds, and take a sup;
And, closely puzzled to agree,
Chatter like gossips over tea.
The gander with his scarlet nose

---

5 John Clare, *Poems, Chiefly from Manuscript*, ed. Edmund Blunden, Alan Porter, Richard Cobden-Sanderson, 1920

When strife's at height will interpose;
And, stretching neck to that and this,
With now a mutter, now a hiss,
A nibble at the feathers too,
A sort of 'pray be quiet do,'
And turning as the matter mends,
He stills them into mutual friends;
Then in a sort of triumph sings
And throws the water o'er his wings.
Ah, could I see a spinney nigh,
A puddock riding in the sky
Above the oaks with easy sail
On stilly wings and forked tail,
Or meet a heath of furze in flower,
I might enjoy a quiet hour,
Sit down at rest, and walk at ease,
And find a many things to please.
But here my fancy's moods admire
The naked levels till they tire,
Nor e'en a molehill cushion meet
To rest on when I want a seat.
Here's little save the river scene
And grounds of oats in rustling green
And crowded growth of wheat and beans,
That with the hope of plenty leans
And cheers the farmer's gazing brow,
Who lives and triumphs in the plough...

ᕱ An Eternal Fierce Destruction

John Keats (1795–1821) was staying in Teignmouth when he penned this extraordinary verse letter to John Hamilton Reynolds in 1818. It describes a dream he had, peopled with famous philosophers in absurd situations; does a riff on Claude Lorrain's painting The Enchanted Castle; *then ends with this startling finale, inspired in part by the sea in the Lorrain painting, in part perhaps by Teignmouth's red-brown cliffs and sandy shore.*

Dear Reynolds! I have a mysterious tale,
And cannot speak it: the first page I read
Upon a lampit rock of green sea-weed
Among the breakers; 'twas a quiet eve,
The rocks were silent, the wide sea did weave
An untumultuous fringe of silver foam
Along the flat brown sand; I was at home
And should have been most happy, – but I saw

Too far into the sea, where every maw
The greater on the less feeds evermore. –
 But I saw too distinct into the core
Of an eternal fierce destruction,
And so from happiness I far was gone.
Still am I sick of it, and tho' to-day,
I've gather'd young spring-leaves, and flowers gay
Of periwinkle and wild strawberry,
Still do I that most fierce destruction see, –
The Shark at savage prey, – the Hawk at pounce, –
The gentle Robin, like a Pard or Ounce,
Ravening a worm, – Away, ye horrid moods!
Moods of one's mind! You know I hate them well.
You know I'd sooner be a clapping Bell
To some Kamtschatkan Missionary Church,
Than with these horrid moods be left i' the lurch.

❧ Darksome Burn

Gerard Manley Hopkins (1844–1889) described his visit to Inversnaid in September 1881 in a letter to a friend: 'I hurried from Glasgow one day to Loch Lomond. The day was dark and partly hid the lake, yet did not altogether disfigure it but gave a pensive or solemn beauty which left a deep impression on me.'

This darksome burn, horseback brown,
His rollrock highroad roaring down,
In coop and in comb the fleece of his foam
Flutes and low to the lake falls home.

A windpuff-bonnet of fawn-froth
Turns and twindles over the broth
Of a pool so pitchblack, fell-frowning,
It rounds and rounds Despair to drowning.

Degged with dew, dappled with dew
Are the groins of the braes that the brook treads through,
Wiry heathpacks, flitches of fern,
And the beadbonny ash that sits over the burn.

What would the world be, once bereft
Of wet and of wildness? Let them be left,
O let them be left, wildness and wet;
Long live the weeds and the wilderness yet.

ᕦ Submarine Gardens

Edmund Gosse (1849–1928) described happy memories of his education in seashore wonders by his normally stern father in his novel Father and Son *(1907).*

It was down on the shore, tramping along the pebbled terraces of the beach, clambering over the great blocks of fallen conglomerate which broke the white curve with rufous promontories that jutted into the sea, or, finally, bending over those shallow tidal pools in the limestone rocks which were our proper hunting-ground, – it was in such circumstances as these that my Father became most easy, most happy, most human. ... Those pools were our mirrors, in which, reflected in the dark hyaline and framed by the sleek and shining fronds of oarweed there used to appear the shapes of a middle-aged man and a funny little boy, equally eager, and, I almost find the presumption to say, equally well prepared for business.

If anyone goes down to those shores now, if man or boy seeks to follow in our traces, let him realize at once, before he takes the trouble to roll up his sleeves, that his zeal will end in labour lost. There is nothing, now, where in our days there was so much. Then the rocks between tide and tide were submarine gardens of a beauty that seemed often to be fabulous, and was positively delusive, since, if we delicately lifted the weed curtains of a windless pool, though we might for a moment see its sides and floor paven with living blossoms, ivory-white, rosy-red, grange and amethyst, yet all that panoply would melt away, furled into the hollow rock, if we so much as dropped a pebble in to disturb the magic dream.

Half a century ago, in many parts of the coast of Devonshire and Cornwall, where the limestone at the water's edge is wrought into crevices and hollows, the tideline was, like Keats' Grecian vase, 'a still unravished bride of quietness'. These cups and basins were always full, whether the tide was high or low, and the only way in which

they were affected was that twice in the twenty-four hours they were replenished by cold streams from the great sea, and then twice were left brimming to be vivified by the temperate movement of the upper air. They were living flower-beds, so exquisite in their perfection, that my Father, in spite of his scientific requirements, used not seldom to pause before he began to rifle them, ejaculating that it was indeed a pity to disturb such congregated beauty. The antiquity of these rock-pools, and the infinite succession of the soft and radiant forms, sea-anemones, seaweeds, shells, fishes, which had inhabited them, undisturbed since the creation of the world, used to occupy my Father's fancy. We burst in, he used to say, where no one had ever thought of intruding before; and if the Garden of Eden had been situated in Devonshire, Adam and Eve, stepping lightly down to bathe in the rainbow-coloured spray, would have seen the identical sights that we now saw, – the great prawns gliding like transparent launches, anthea waving in the twilight its thick white waxen tentacles, and the fronds of the dulse faintly streaming on the water like huge red banners in some reverted atmosphere.

❧ Fleecy Fall

Thomas Hardy turned to writing poetry after growing criticism of his doom-laden novels. His poems reflect his concerns in a rapidly changing world: 'Snow in the Suburbs', which appeared in his Collected Poems *(1919) is not just a beautiful description of snow but an appeal for the 'loving kindness' that he thought was humankind's only defence against an indifferent universe.*

Every branch big with it,
Bent every twig with it;
Every fork like a white web-foot;
Every street and pavement mute:
Some flakes have lost their way, and grope back upward when
Meeting those meandering down they turn and descend again.
The palings are glued together like a wall,
And there is no waft of wind with the fleecy fall.

A sparrow enters the tree,
Whereon immediately
A snow-lump thrice his own slight size
Descends on him and showers his head and eye
And overturns him,
And near inurns him,
And lights on a nether twig, when its brush
Starts off a volley of other lodging lumps with a rush.

The steps are a blanched slope,
Up which, with feeble hope,
A black cat comes, wide-eyed and thin;
And we take him in.

❧ Old Father Beaver

Grey Owl was the pen-name of the trapper-turned-conservationist Archibald Belaney (1888–1938). This description of beavers is from his best-selling children's novel, The Adventures of Sajo and Her Beaver People *(1935).*

The pond was bright with sunshine; very silent and peaceful it was, back there among the Hills of the Whispering Leaves, and so calm, that the few ducks dozing quietly upon its waters seemed almost to be floating on air, and the slim white poplar trees that stood upon its banks were reflected so plainly on its smooth surface, that it was hard to tell where the water stopped and the trees began. It was very beautiful, like a fairy-land, with its silver poplars and May flowers and blue water. And it was very still, for nothing moved there, and it seemed quite lifeless except for the sleeping ducks. Yet, had you watched patiently for a little while, being careful not to move or talk, or even whisper, you would have seen, before very long, a ripple on the water near the shore as a dark brown head, with round ears that showed very plainly, peered cautiously out from the rushes at the water's edge, and watched and listened and sniffed. The head was followed by a furry body, as its owner now came out in full sight and swam rapidly, but without a sound, to another place on the far shore, there to disappear among the reeds. The tall reeds swayed and shook for a minute as he worked there, and then he reappeared, this time holding before him a large bundle of grass, and swam over towards an enormous black mound of earth that we had been wondering about all this time, and dived, bundle and all, right in front of it. He had scarcely disappeared before another head, with another bundle, could be seen swimming from a different direction when – somebody moved, and with no warning at all, a huge flat tail came down on the water with a heavy smack, and with a mighty splash and a plunge the head and its bundle were gone. Now, this was exactly what had happened to Big Feather, down on the river that morning,

Thierleben
von A. E. Brehm

and for the same reason. For that great mound, taller than any of us, before which the swimmers had dived, was a beaver house, and the dark brown, furry heads were those of the Beaver People themselves. And they had been very busy.

The lodge had been built up to more than six feet in height, and was a good ten feet across. It had lately been well plastered with wet mud, and heavy billets of wood had been laid on the slopes of it to hold everything firmly in place. It all looked very strong and safe-looking, like a fortress, and even a moose could have walked around on top of it without doing it a bit of harm. Up the side of it there was a wide pathway, on which the building materials were carried, and had you been more patient or careful awhile ago, or perhaps had the wind not played a trick on you and given you away to those keen noses, you might have seen old father beaver dig out a load of earth from the shore, go with it to the house, swimming slowly and carefully so as not to lose any, and then, standing upright like a man, walk to the top of the roof with the load in his arms and there dump it, pushing it into nooks and crannies with his hands, and shoving a good-sized stick in after it to keep it there.

And all this work had been done with a purpose. It was a very important time, this Month of Flowers, for inside that queer-looking home, hidden away from the eyes of all the world, were four tiny little kitten beavers. Woolly little fellows they were, perfectly formed, with bright black eyes, big webbed hind feet, little hand-like fore-paws and tiny, flat, rubbery-looking tails. They had marvellous appetites, and their lungs must have been very good too, for they were the noisiest little creatures imaginable.

ᔮ Sea Music

Henry Beston (1888–1968) retreated to Cape Cod in 1925 to live in a 20'x16' shack he called The Fo'castle. The fruit of his stay there was the nature classic The Outermost House: A Year of Life on the Great Beach of Cape Cod *(1928). It had a lasting impact on Rachel Carson, author of* The Silent Spring *(1962).*

The three great elemental sounds in nature are the sound of rain, the sound of wind in a primeval wood, and the sound of outer ocean on a beach. I have heard them all, and of the three elemental voices, that of ocean is the most awesome, beautiful, and varied. For it is a mistake to talk of the monotone of ocean or of the monotonous nature of its sound.

The sea has many voices. Listen to the surf – really lend it your ears – and you will hear in it a world of sounds: hollow boomings and heavy roarings, great watery tumblings and tramplings, long hissing seethes, sharp rifle-shot reports, splashes, whispers, the grinding undertone of stones, and sometimes vocal sounds that might be the halfheard talk of people in the sea. And not only is the great sound varied in the manner of its making, it is also constantly changing its tempo, its pitch, its accent, and its rhythm, being now loud and thundering, now almost placid, now furious, now grave and solemn-slow, now a simple measure, now a rhythm monstrous with a sense of purpose and elemental will.

Every mood of the wind, every change in the day's weather, every phase of the tide – all these have subtle sea musics all their own. Surf of the ebb, for instance, is one music, surf of the flood another, the change in the two musics being most clearly marked during the first hour of a rising tide. With the renewal of the tidal energy, the sound of the surf grows louder, the fury of battle returns to it as it turns again on the land, and beat and sound change with the renewal of the war.

The seas are the heart's blood of the earth. Plucked up and kneaded by the sun and the moon, the tides are systole and diastole of earth's veins.

The rhythm of waves beats in the sea like a pulse in living flesh. It is pure force, forever embodying itself in a succession of watery shapes which vanish on its passing.

☙ Like a Great Sigh

Henry Williamson (1895–1977) moved to the North Devon coast in 1921, and discovered the setting for his famous Tarka the Otter: His Joyful Water-life and Death in the Two Rivers *(1927). This passage from the book that made his name sets the swallows' imminent migration against the coming end of Tarka's childhood, and shows the intensity of Williamson's writing.*

On the fourth night of the otters' arrival at the Ram's-horn duck-pond, the swallows which settled among the reed-maces at sunset didn't sleep. They twittered among themselves when the first stars gleamed in the water, for they had received a sign to leave the green meadows they loved so well. They talked in their undersong voices – which men seldom hear, they are so soft and sweet – while clinging to the unburst heads of the reed-maces. They talked of white-and-grey seas, of winds that fling away the stroke of wings, of great thunder-shocks in the sun-whitened clouds under, of wild rains and hunger and fatigue to come before they saw again the sparkles in the foam of the African strand. But none talked of the friends who would fall in the sea, or be slain in France and Spain and Italy, or break their necks against the glass of lighthouses, for the fork-tailed birds of summer had no thought of these things, or of death. They were joyous and pure in spirit, and alien to the ways of man.

During the day Tarka had been watching them, being curious. He had watched them sweeping above him with a windy rush of wings that darkened the sky and splashed in the wind-ruffled water. As he was stretching himself before leaving his couch at sunset, they flew up like a great sigh up to the stars. Krark! Krark! Krark! cried old Nog the heron, standing grave and still in the shallow water at the pond's edge. It was the last English voice many of them would hear, the blue winged ones of summer, who had begun the weary migration from the land of thatched homesteads and old cob linhays.

Some days after the swallows had gone, Tarka heard a short,

soft, mellow whistle while playing in the Ram's-horn duckpond. The five otters ceased their play and listened. The whistle came again, and Tarka's mother answered. The answering whistle was keen and loud. The bitch swam towards it, followed by Greymuzzle and White-tip. The whistle made Tarka cry in rage, Ic-yang, and when a dog-cub has cried thus, he is no more a cub, but an otter.

❧ Ten Per Cent God

Kenneth Steven (b. 1968) concentrates all the magic of otters into the eight lines of his poem 'The Small Giant'. From Iona *(2000).*

The otter is ninety per cent water
Ten per cent God.

This is a mastery
We have not fathomed in a million years.

I saw one once, off the teeth of western Scotland.
Playing games with the Atlantic –

Three feet of gymnastics
Taking on an ocean

ᴈ In Passage

Graeme Stones (b. 1956) once worked on oilrigs; he now lives and works and writes on the Isle of Luing. This unpublished poem is printed with his kind permission.

Up the sternramp humped
A seal pup, storm-orphaned,
Irate
As a baited badger

Scooped from the swell
A drowning guillemot,
Shapeless, little more
Than a clot of crude
But for the dark blink
Of an eye.

Strangest of all at dawn the deck
Littered with goldcrests
Three hundred miles from leaf
Or perch, foreheads blazing minutely
Indifferent to crumbs
And stiff by noon.

For all of these our ship
Like our concern
Not of their element.

Surprise

What is this life if, full of care,
We have no time to stand and stare.
No time to stand beneath the boughs
And stare as long as sheep or cows.

W H Davies, 'Leisure', *Songs of Joy and Others*, 1911

⚘ Mighty Strifes

Pliny the Elder (AD 23–79) was a renowned naturalist, but he seems to have been somewhat gullible, particularly in his account in his Natural History *(Book VIII, ch. 11–12) of the perpetual war waged between Indian elephants and dragons.*

Africa produces elephants, beyond the deserts of the Syrtes, and in Mauritania; they are found also in the countries of the Æthiopians and the Troglodytæ as mentioned above. But it is India that produces the largest, as well as the dragon, which is perpetually at war with the elephant, and is itself of so enormous a size, as easily to envelope the elephants with its folds, and encircle them in its coils. The contest is equally fatal to both; the elephant, vanquished, falls to the earth, and by its weight, crushes the dragon which is entwined around it.

The sagacity which every animal exhibits in its own behalf is wonderful, but in these it is remarkably so. The dragon has much

difficulty in climbing up to so great a height, and therefore, watching the road, which bears marks of their footsteps when going to feed, it darts down upon them from a lofty tree. The elephant knows that it is quite unable to struggle against the folds of the serpent, and so seeks for trees or rocks against which to rub itself.

The dragon is on its guard against this, and tries to prevent it, by first of all confining the legs of the elephant with the folds of its tail; while the elephant, on the other hand, endeavours to disengage itself with its trunk. The dragon, however, thrusts its head into its nostrils, and thus, at the same moment, stops the breath and wounds the most tender parts.

When it is met unexpectedly, the dragon raises itself up, faces its opponent, and flies more especially at the eyes; this is the reason why elephants are so often found blind, and worn to a skeleton with hunger and misery. What other cause can one assign for such mighty strifes as these, except that Nature is desirous, as it were, to make an exhibition for herself, in pitting such opponents against each other?

ᶜᵒ Tree Geese

John Gerard (1545–1612) followed early naturalists like Aristotle, Pliny and Frederick Hohenzollern in describing geese that hatched from trees in the Orkney Islands and Lancashire in his Herbal, or General History of Plants *(1597).*

There are found in the North parts of Scotland and the Island adjacent, called Orchades, certain trees whereon do grow certain shells of a white colour tending to russet, wherein are contained little living creatures, which shells in time of maturity do open, and out of them do grow those little living things, which falling in the water do become fowls, which we call Barnacles ... but the other that do fall upon the land perish and come to nothing. Thus much by the writings of others, and also from the mouths of people of those parts, which may very well accord with truth.

But what our eyes have seen and hands have touched we shall declare. There is a small Island in Lancashire called the Pile of Foulders [Piel Island, off Furness] wherein are found the broken pieces of old and bruised ships, somewhere of have been cast thither

by shipwreck, and also the trunks and bodies with the branches of old and rotten trees cast up there likewise; whereon is found a certain spume or froth that in time breedeth unto certain shells in shape like those of the Mussel, but sharper pointed and of a whitish colour, wherein is contained a thing in form like a lace of silk finely woven as it were together, one end thereof is fastened unto the belly of a rude mass or lump, which in time cometh to the shape and form of a Bird. When it is perfectly formed the shell gapeth open, and the first thing that appeareth is the foresaid lace or string; next come the legs of the bird hanging out, and as it groweth greater it openeth the shell by degrees until at length it is all come forth and hangeth only by the bill; in short space after it cometh to full maturity and falleth into the sea, where it gathereth feathers and groweth to a fowl bigger than a Mallard and lesser than a goose, having black legs, and bill and beak, and feathers black and white spotted in such manner as is our magpie, which the people of Lancashire call by no other name than a tree goose: which place aforesaid and all those parts adjoining do so much abound therein that one of the best is bought for threepence. For the truth hereof, if any doubt, may it please them to repair unto me, and I shall satisfy them by the testimony of good witnesses.

ᘓ Spaniels, Mastiffs and Dancers

William Harrison (1534–1593) drew the fascinating information about dogs in the third book of his Description of England *(1577) partly from classical authorities, but mainly from the treatise published in Latin on the subject in 1570 by Dr John Caius of Cambridge, who is the 'he' referred to in the text.*

There is no country that may (as I take it) compare with ours in number, excellency, and diversity of dogs. The first sort divideth either into such as rouse the beast, and continue the chase, or springeth the bird, and bewrayeth her flight by pursuit. And as these are commonly called spaniels, so the other are named hounds, whereof he maketh eight sorts, of which the foremost excelleth in perfect smelling, the second in quick espying, the third in swiftness and quickness, the fourth in smelling and nimbleness, etc., and the last in subtlety and deceitfulness. These (saith Strabo) are most apt for game, and called Sagaces by a general name, not only because of their skill in hunting, but also for that they know their own and the names of their fellows most exactly. For if the hunter see any one to follow skilfully, and with likelihood of good success, he biddeth the rest to hark and follow such a dog, and they eftsoons obey so soon as they hear his name. The first kind of these are often called harriers, whose game is the fox, the hare, the wolf (if we had any), hart, buck, badger, otter, polecat, lopstart, weasel, coney, etc.; the second height a terrier, and it hunteth the badger and grey only; the third a bloodhound, whose office is to follow the fierce, and now and then to pursue a thief or beast by his dry foot; the fourth height a gazehound, who hunteth by the eye; the fifth a greyhound, cherished for his strength and swiftness and stature, … of which sort also some be smooth, of sundry colours, and some shake-haired; the sixth a lymer, that excelleth in smelling and swift running; the seventh a tumbler; and the eighth a thief whose offices … incline only to deceit, wherein they are oft so skilful

that few men would think so mischievous a wit to remain in such silly creatures.

Having made this enumeration of dogs which are apt for the chase and hunting, he cometh next to such as serve the falcons in their time, whereof he maketh also two sorts. One that findeth his game on the land, another that putteth up such fowl as keepeth in the water: and of these this is commonly most usual for the net or train, the other for the hawk, as he doth shew at large. Of the first he saith that they have no peculiar names assigned to them severally, but each of them is called after the bird which by natural appointment he is allotted to hunt or serve, for which consideration some be named dogs for the pheasant, some for the falcon, and some for the partridge. Howbeit the common name for all is spaniel (saith he), and thereupon alluded as if these kinds of dogs had been brought hither out of Spain. In like sort we have of water spaniels in their kind.

The third sort of dogs of the gentle kind is the spaniel gentle, or comforter, or (as the common term is) the fisting-hound, and those are called Melitei, of the Island Malta, from whence they were brought hither. These are little and pretty, proper and fine, and sought out far and near to falsify the nice delicacy of dainty dames, and wanton women's wills, instruments of folly to play and dally withal, in trifling away the treasure of time, to withdraw their minds from more commendable exercises, and to content their corrupt concupiscences with vain disport – a silly poor shift to shun their irksome idleness. These Sybaritical puppies the smaller they be (and thereto if they have a hole in the fore parts of their heads) the better they are accepted, the more pleasure also they provoke, as meet playfellows for mincing mistresses to bear in their bosoms, to keep company withal in their chambers, to succour with sleep in bed, and nourish with meat at board, to lie in their laps, and lick their lips as they lie (like young Dianas) in their waggons and coaches. And good reason it should be so, for coarseness with fineness hath no fellowship, but featness with neatness hath neighbourhood enough. ...

Dogs of the homely kind are either shepherd's curs or mastiffs. The first are so common that it needeth me not to speak of them. Their use also is so well known in keeping the herd together (either when they grass or go before the shepherd) that it should be but in vain to spend any time about them. Wherefore I will leave this cur unto his own kind, and go in hand with the mastiff, tie dog, or band dog, so called because many of them are tied up in chains and strong bonds in the daytime, for doing hurt abroad, which is a huge dog, stubborn, ugly, eager, burthenous of body (and therefore of but little swiftness), terrible and fearful to behold, and oftentimes more fierce and fell than any Archadian or Corsican cur. Our Englishmen, to the extent that these dogs may be more cruel and fierce, assist nature with some art, use, and custom. For although this kind of dog be capable of courage, violent, valiant, stout, and bold: yet will they increase these their stomachs by teaching them to bait the bear, the bull, the lion, and other such like cruel and bloody beasts (either brought over or kept up at home for the same purpose), without any collar to defend their throats, and oftentimes there too they train them up in fighting and wrestling with a man (having for the safe-guard of his life either a pikestaff, club, sword, privy coat), whereby they become the more fierce and cruel unto strangers. ...

The force which is in them surmounteth all belief, and the fast hold which they take with their teeth exceedeth all credit: for three of them against a bear, four against a lion, are sufficient to try mastries with them. King Henry the Seventh, as the report goeth, commanded all such curs to be hanged, because they durst presume to fight against the lion, who is their king and sovereign. ...

Some of them moreover will suffer a stranger to come in and walk about the house or yard where he listeth, without giving over to follow him: but if he put forth his hand to touch anything, then will they fly upon them and kill them if they may. I had one myself once, which would not suffer any man to bring in his weapon further than my gate: neither those that were of my house to be touched in his presence. Or if I had beaten any of my children, he would gently have essayed to catch the rod in his teeth and take it out of my hand or else pluck down their clothes to save them from the stripes: which in my opinion is not unworthy to be noted.

The last sort of dogs consisteth of the currish kind meet for many toys, of which the whappet or prick-eared cur is one. Some men call them warners, because they are good for nothing else but to bark and give warning when anybody doth stir or lie in wait about the house in the night season. Certes it is impossible to describe these curs in any order, because they have no one kind proper unto themselves, but are a confused company mixed of all the rest. The second sort of them are called turnspits, whose office is not unknown to any. And as these are only reserved for this purpose, so in many places our mastiffs (beside the use which tinkers have of them in carrying their heavy budgets) are made to draw water in great wheels out of deep wells, going much like unto those which are framed for our turnspits, as is to be seen at Royston ...

The last kind of toyish curs are named dancers, and those being of a mongrel sort also, are taught and exercised to dance in measure at the musical sound of an instrument, as at the just stroke of a drum, sweet accent of the citharne, and pleasant harmony of the harp, shewing many tricks by the gesture of their bodies: as to stand bolt upright, to lie flat on the ground, to turn round as a ring holding their tails in their teeth, to saw and beg for meat, to take a man's cap from his head, and sundry such properties, which they learn of their idle roguish masters, whose instruments they are to gather gain, as old apes clothed in motley and coloured short-waisted jackets are for the like vagabonds...

⚕ Creatures of Habit

Gilbert White (1720–1793) enjoyed reporting on the resourcefulness of swallows in his Natural History of Selborne *(1789).*

A certain swallow built for two years together on the handles of a pair of garden shears that were stuck up against the boards in an out-house, and therefore must have her nest spoiled whenever that implement was wanted; and what is stranger still, another bird of the same species built its nest on the wings and body of an owl that happened by accident to hang dead and dry from the rafter of a barn. This owl, with the nest on its wings, and with eggs in the nest, was brought as a curiosity worthy of the most elegant private museum in Great Britain. The owner, struck with the oddity of the sight, furnished the bringer with a large shell or conch, desiring him to fix it just where the owl hung: the person did as he was ordered, and the following year, a pair, probably the same pair, built their nest in the conch and laid their eggs.

⤳ The Things With Yellow Heads

*George Crabbe (1754–1832) was an observant naturalist and a keen ento-
mologist. In 'The Preceptor Husband', from* Tales of the Hall *(1819), he
makes rueful fun of a husband's attempt to educate his romance-loving wife
in plant science.*

They walked at leisure through their wood and groves,
In fields and lanes, and talked of plants and loves,
And loves of plants. Said Finch, 'Augusta, dear,
You said you loved to learn, – were you sincere?
Do you remember that you told me once
How much you grieved, and said you were a dunce?
That is, you wanted information. Say,
What would you learn? I will direct your way.'

'Goodness', said she, 'what meanings you discern
In a few words! I said I wished to learn,
And so I think I did; and you replied,
The wish was good: what would you now beside?
Did not you say it showed an ardent mind;
And pray what more do you expect to find?'

'My dear Augusta, could you wish indeed
For any knowledge, and not then proceed?
That is not wishing' –
                                        – 'Mercy! how you tease!'
You knew I said it with a view to please;
A compliment to you, and quite enough, –
You would not kill me with that puzzling stuff!
'Sure I might say I wish'd; but that is still
Far from a promise: it is not, "I will".

But come, to show you that I will not hide
My proper talents, you shall be my guide;
And Lady Boothby, when we meet, shall cry,
"She's quite as good a botanist as I'".

'Right, my Augusta'; and, in manner grave,
Finch his first lecture on the science gave;
An introduction, – and he said, 'My dear,
Your thought was happy, – let us persevere;
And let no trifling cause our work retard', –
Agreed the lady, but she fear'd it hard.

Now o'er the grounds they rambled many a mile;
He showed the flowers, the stamina, the style,
Calix and corol, pericarp and fruit,
And all the plant produces, branch and root;
Of these he treated, every varying shape,
Till poor Augusta panted to escape:
He showed the various foliage plants produce,
Lunate and lyrate, runcinate, retuse;
Long were the learned words, and urged with force,
Panduriform, pinnatifid, premorse,
Latent, and patent, papulous, and plane, –
'Oh!' said the pupil, 'it will turn my brain.'
'Fear not', he answer'd, and again, intent
To fill that mind, o'er class and order went;
And stopping, 'Now,' said he, 'my love, attend.'
'I do,' said she, 'but when will be an end?'
'When we have made some progress, – now begin,
Which is the stigma, show me with the pin:
Come, I have told you, dearest, let me see,
Times very many, – tell it now to me.'

'Stigma! I know, – the things with yellow heads,
That shed the dust, and grow upon the threads;
You call them wives and husbands, but you know
That is a joke – here, look, and I will show
All I remember.' – Doleful was the look
Of the preceptor, when he shut his book,
(The system brought to aid them in their view,)
And now with sighs return'd – 'It will not do.'

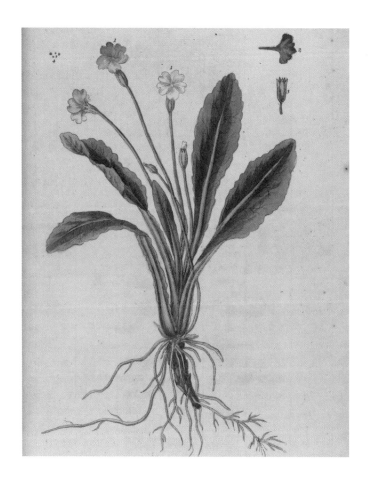

ᴥ The Naturalist and the Poet

Dorothy Wordsworth (1771–1855) needed no education as an observer. When she and William went for a walk along the shores of Ullswater on a stormy day, and saw daffodils tossed by the wind, Dorothy recorded the occasion in her journal with her customary minute accuracy and fine sensibility.

Thursday 15th. When we were in the woods beyond Gowbarrow Park we saw a few daffodils close to the water side. We fancied that the lake had floated the seeds ashore and that the little colony had so sprung up. But as we went along there were more and yet more and at last under the boughs of the trees, we saw that there was a long belt of them along the shore, about the breadth of a country turnpike road. I never saw daffodils so beautiful; they grew among the mossy stones about and about them, some rested their heads upon these stones as on a pillow for weariness and the rest tossed and reeled and danced and seemed as if they verily laughed with the wind that blew upon them over the lake, they looked so gay ever glancing ever changing. The wind blew directly over the lake to them. There was here and there a little knot and a few stragglers a few yards higher up but they were so few as not to disturb the simplicity and unity and life of that one busy highway.

William seems to have read her impressions before he penned his famous poem in memory of the flowers; he also erased her from the picture.

> I wandered lonely as a cloud
> That floats on high o'er vales and hills,
> When all at once I saw a crowd,
> A host, of golden daffodils;
> Beside the lake, beneath the trees,
> Fluttering and dancing in the breeze.

Continuous as the stars that shine
And twinkle on the milky way,
They stretched in never-ending line
Along the margin of a bay:
Ten thousand saw I at a glance,
Tossing their heads in sprightly dance.

The waves beside them danced; but they
Out-did the sparkling waves in glee:
A poet could not but be gay,
In such a jocund company:
I gazed – and gazed– but little thought
What wealth the show to me had brought:

For oft, when on my couch I lie
In vacant or in pensive mood,
They flash upon that inward eye
Which is the bliss of solitude;
And then my heart with pleasure fills,
And dances with the daffodils.

ᘓ Belling the Rat

Jane Loudon (1807–1858) was an early pioneer of science fiction, who also wrote popular gardening manuals. She revised Thomas Boreman's 1736 Description of a Great Variety of Animals and Vegetables *and published it as* Mrs Loudon's Entertaining Naturalist Being Popular Descriptions, Tales, And Anecdotes of more than Five Hundred Animals *(1850). Among them is an unusual approach to deterring rats.*

The Rat (*Mus decumanus*) is about four times as large as the mouse, but of a dusky colour, with white under the body; his head is longer, his neck shorter, and his eyes comparatively larger. These animals are so attached to our dwellings, that it is almost impossible to destroy the breed, when they have once taken a liking to any particular place. Their produce is enormous, as they have from ten to twenty young ones at a litter, and this thrice a year. Thus their increase is such, that it is possible for a single pair (supposing food to be sufficiently plentiful, and that they had no enemies to lessen their numbers) to amount at the end of two years to upwards of a million;

Werner pinx. et del.   ⅔ de la grand. nat.   Lithog. de C. de Last

but an insatiable appetite impels them to destroy each other; the weaker always fall a prey to the stronger; and the large male Rat, which usually lives by itself, is dreaded by those of its own species as their most formidable enemy.

The rat is a bold and fierce little animal, and when closely pursued, will turn and fasten on its assailant. Its bite is keen, and the wound it inflicts is painful and difficult to heal, owing to the form of its teeth, which are long, sharp, and of an irregular form. It digs with great facility and vigour, making its way with rapidity beneath the floors of our houses, between the stones and bricks of walls, and often excavating the foundations of a dwelling to a dangerous extent. There are many instances of their totally undermining the most solid mason-work, or burrowing through dams which had for ages served to confine the waters of rivers and canals.

A gentleman, some time ago, travelling through Mecklenburgh, was witness to a very singular circumstance respecting one of these animals, in the post-house at New Hargarel. After dinner, the land-lord placed on the floor a large dish of soup, and gave a loud whistle. Immediately there came into the room a mastiff, an Angora cat, an old raven, and a large Rat with a bell about its neck. They all four went to the dish, and without disturbing each other, fed together; after which, the dog, cat, and rat lay before the fire, while the raven hopped about the room. The landlord, after accounting for the familiarity which existed among these animals, informed his guest that the rat was the most useful of the four; for that the noise he made had completely freed the house from the rats and mice with which it had been before infested.

❦ Dressing the Part

Margaret Gatty (1809–1873) advises aspiring female naturalists on dress in the introduction to her History of British Seaweeds *(1863).*

Lay aside, for a time, all thought of conventional appearances and be content to support the weight of a pair of boy's shooting boots, which furthermore, should be rendered as waterproof as possible by receiving a thin coat of neat's-foot oil, such as is used by fishermen – a process well understood in most lodging houses … Next to boots comes the question of petticoats; and if anything could excuse a woman from imitating the costume of a man, it would be what she suffers as a seaweed collector from these necessary draperies! But to make the best of a bad matter, let woollen be in the ascendant as much as possible; and let the petticoats never come below the ankle.

A ladies' yachting costume has come into fashion of late, which is perhaps as near perfection for shore-work as anything that could be devised. It is a suit consisting of a full short skirt of blue flannel or serge (like very fine bathing gown material), with waistcoat and jacket to match. Cloaks and shawls which necessarily hamper the arms, besides having long ends and corners, which cannot fail to get soaked, are, of course, very inconvenient, and should be as much avoided as possible; but where this cannot be, a good deal may be done towards tucking them neatly up out of the way.

In conclusion, a hat is preferable to bonnet, merino stockings to cotton ones, and a strong pair of gloves is indispensable. All millinery work, silks, satins, lace, bracelets and other jewellery etc. must, and will be, laid aside by every rational being who attempts to shore-hunt … But even in reflecting on the best and easiest shore … it must be owned that a low-water-mark expedition, is more comfortably undertaken under the protection of a gentleman. He may fossilise, or sketch, or even (if he will be savage and barbaric) shoot gulls; but no need anyhow to involve him in the messing after what he may consider 'rubbish', unless happily, he be inclined to assist. Only let there be sea and plenty of low, dark rock.

✆ All the Wealth of Pomona

Henry David Thoreau (1817–1862) is most famous for Walden *(1854), the story of his sojourn in the forest. Less known is his charming and learned essay in praise of apple trees and their fruits, 'Wild Apples', which was published in* Atlantic Monthly *in 1862.*

The flowers of the apple are perhaps the most beautiful of any tree, so copious and so delicious to both sight and scent. The walker is frequently tempted to turn and linger near some more than usually handsome one, whose blossoms are two thirds expanded. How superior it is in these respects to the pear, whose blossoms are neither coloured nor fragrant!

By the middle of July, green apples are so large as to remind us of coddling [ie cooking them], and of the autumn. The sward is commonly strewed with little ones which fall still-born, as it were, – Nature thus thinning them for us. The Roman writer Palladius said: 'If apples are inclined to fall before their time, a stone placed in a split root will retain them.' Some such notion, still surviving, may account for some of the stones which we see placed to be overgrown in the forks of trees. They have a saying in Suffolk, England, 'At Michaelmas time, or a little before, Half an apple goes to the core.'

Early apples begin to be ripe about the first of August; but I think that none of them are so good to eat as some to smell. One is worth more to scent your handkerchief with than any perfume which they sell in the shops. The fragrance of some fruits is not to be forgotten, along with that of flowers. Some gnarly apple which I pick up in the road reminds me by its fragrance of all the wealth of Pomona [the Roman goddess of fruit and fruit trees] – carrying me forward to those days when they will be collected in golden and ruddy heaps in the orchards and about the cider-mills. ...

In October, the leaves falling, the apples are more distinct on the trees. I saw one year in a neighbouring town some trees fuller of

fruit than I remember to have ever seen before, small yellow apples hanging over the road. The branches were gracefully drooping with their weight, like a barberry-bush, so that the whole tree acquired a new character. Even the topmost branches, instead of standing erect, spread and drooped in all directions; and there were so many poles supporting the lower ones, that they looked like pictures of banyan-trees. As an old English manuscript says, 'The mo appelen the tree bereth the more sche boweth to the folk.' ...

Cool evenings prompt the farmers to make haste, and at length I see only the ladders here and there left leaning against the trees. It would be well if we accepted these gifts with more joy and gratitude, and did not think it enough simply to put a fresh load of compost about the tree. Some old English customs are suggestive at least. I find them described chiefly in Brand's Popular Antiquities. It appears that 'on Christmas Eve the farmers and their men in Devonshire take a large bowl of cider, with a toast in it, and carrying it in state to the orchard, they salute the apple-trees with much ceremony, in order to make them bear well the next season.' This salutation consists in 'throwing some of the cider about the roots of the tree, placing bits of the toast on the branches,' and then, 'encircling one of the best bearing trees in the orchard, they drink the following toast three several times:–

"Here's to thee, old apple-tree,
Whence thou mayst bud, and whence thou mayst blow,
And whence thou mayst bear apples enow!
Hats-full! caps-full!
Bushel, bushel, sacks-full!
And my pockets full, too!
Hurrah!'"

☞ What Looking-glass Insects Eat

Lewis Carroll (1832–1898) parodies the earnest nature study that was so much part of Victorian childhoods in Through The Looking Glass and What Alice Found There *(1871).*

'All right,' said the Gnat: 'half way up that bush, you'll see a Rocking-horse-fly, if you look. It's made entirely of wood, and gets about by swinging itself from branch to branch.'

'What does it live on?' Alice asked, with great curiosity.

'Sap and sawdust,' said the Gnat. 'Go on with the list.'

Alice looked up at the Rocking-horse-fly with great interest, and made up her mind that it must have been just repainted, it looked so bright and sticky; and then she went on.

'And there's the Dragon-fly.'

'Look on the branch above your head,' said the Gnat, 'and there you'll find a snap-dragon-fly. Its body is made of plum-pudding,

its wings of holly-leaves, and its head is a raisin burning in brandy.'

'And what does it live on?'

'Frumenty and mince pie,' the Gnat replied; 'and it makes its nest in a Christmas box.'

'And then there's the Butterfly,' Alice went on, after she had taken a good look at the insect with its head on fire, and had thought to herself, 'I wonder if that's the reason insects are so fond of flying into candles – because they want to turn into Snap-dragon-flies!'

'Crawling at your feet,' said the Gnat (Alice drew her feet back in some alarm), 'you may observe a Bread-and-Butterfly. Its wings are thin slices of Bread-and-butter, its body is a crust, and its head is a lump of sugar.'

'And what does IT live on?'

'Weak tea with cream in it.'

A new difficulty came into Alice's head. 'Supposing it couldn't find any?' she suggested.

'Then it would die, of course.'

'But that must happen very often,' Alice remarked thoughtfully.

'It always happens,' said the Gnat.

✧ Highly Flavoured Game

Jean-Henri Fabré (1823–1915) was a self-taught French entomologist who had a direct and lively style derived from his life as a teacher. He specialised in an informally biographical approach, as in The Life of the Grasshopper *(1917).*

It is near the end of August, the male, that slender swain, thinks the moment propitious. He makes eyes at his strapping companion; he turns his head in her direction; he bends his neck and throws out his chest. His little pointed face wears an almost impassioned expression. Motionless, in this posture, for a long time he contemplates the object of his desire. She does not stir, is as though indifferent. The lover, however, has caught a sign of acquiescence, a sign of which I do not know the secret. He goes nearer; suddenly he spreads his wings, which quiver with a convulsive tremor. That is his declaration. He rushes, small as he is, upon the back of his corpulent companion, clings on as best he can, steadies his hold. As a rule, the preliminaries last a long time. At last, coupling takes place and is also long drawn out, lasting sometimes for five or six hours. Nothing worthy of attention happens between the two motionless partners. They end by separating, but only to unite again in a more intimate fashion. If the poor fellow is loved by his lady as the vivifier of her ovaries, he is also loved as a piece of highly-flavoured game. And, that same day, or at latest on the morrow, he is seized by his spouse, who first gnaws his neck, in accordance with precedent, and then eats him deliberately, by little mouthfuls, leaving only the wings.

↩ The Lonely Swan and the Trout

*W H Hudson (1841–1922) was born in Buenos Aires, but settled in England
in 1894, where he became an ardent naturalist. He was a founder member
of the Royal Society for the Protection of Birds. This extract is from his*
Adventures Among Birds *(1913).*

Another even stranger case must be told in conclusion – the sad
case of a lonely swan in search of a friend, and as it is a story of the
'incredible' sort I am glad I have permission to give the names of the
persons who witnessed the affair. The place is Little Chelmsford Hall,
near Chelmsford, and the witnesses are Lady Pennefather and her
friend Miss Guinness who resides with her. Near the house there is
an artificial lake of considerable length, fed by a stream which flows
into the grounds on one side and out at the other. Lake and stream
are stocked with trout. A pair of swans are kept on the lake and
three or four years ago they reared a single young one, which after
some months when it was fully grown they began to persecute. The
young swan, however, could not endure to be alone, and although
driven furiously off to a distance a hundred times a day he would
still return. Eventually he was punished so mercilessly that he gave
it up and went right away to the further end of the lake and made
that part his home.

About this time Miss Guinness started making a series of water-
colour sketches at that end of the lake, and her presence was a
happiness to the swan. Invariably on her appearance he would start
swimming rapidly towards her, then leaving the water he would
follow her about until she sat down to do a sketch, whereupon the
swan would settle itself by her side to stay contentedly with her until
she finished. This went on for five or six weeks till the sketching
was done and Miss Guinness went away on a visit. Again the poor
bird was alone and miserable until a man was sent to work in the
shrubbery by the lake, and at once the swan made a companion

of him; each morning it would come from the lake to meet him, to spend the whole day in his company. In due time the work was finished and the man went away. Once more the swan was miserable, and it made the lady of the house unhappy to see it, so anxious appeared the bird to be with her whenever she went near the lake, so distressed when she left it.

All at once there was a change in its behaviour; it was no longer waiting and watching for a visitor to the lake-side and ready to leave the water on her appearance. It now appeared quite contented to be alone and would rest on the water at the same spot for an hour at a time, floating motionless or else propelling itself with such a slow and gentle movement of its oars as to make it appear almost stationary. It was an astonishing change but a welcome one, as the unhappiness of the swan had begun to make everybody feel bad, and now it looked as if the poor bird had become reconciled to a solitary life. A little later the reason of this change appeared when the extraordinary discovery was made that the swan was not alone after all, that he had a friend who was constantly with him – a big trout! The fish had his place at the side of the bird, just below the surface, and together they would rest and together move like one being. Those who first saw it could hardly credit the evidence of their own senses, but in a short time they became convinced that this amazing thing had come to pass, that these two ill-assorted beings had actually become companions.

How can we explain it? The swan, we have seen, was in a state of misery at his isolation and doubtless ready to attach himself to and find a solace in the company of any living creature on land or in the water, and a fish happened to be the only creature there. But how about the trout? I can only suppose that he got some profit out of the partnership, that the swan when feeding by the margin accidentally fed the trout by shaking small insects into the water, and that in this way the swan became associated with food in what we are pleased to call the trout's mind. The biologist denies that it – the poor fish – has a mind at all, since it has no cortex to its brain, but we need not trouble ourselves with this question just now. I also think it possible that the swan may have touched or stroked the back of his strange friend with his beak, just as one swan would caress another swan, and that this contact was grateful to the trout. Fish have as much delight in being gently stroked as other creatures that wear a skin or scales. I have picked up many 'wild worms in woods' and many a wild toad, if wild toads there be, and have quickly over come their wildness and made them contented to be in my hands by gently stroking them on the back.

The sequel remains to be told. There came to the Hall a visitor from London, who being a keen angler got up very early in the morning and went to the lake to try and get a trout for break-fast. About eight o'clock he returned and finding his hostess down proudly exhibited to her a magnificent trout he had caught. He had not looked for such a big one, and he would never forget catching this particular trout for another reason. A wonderful thing had happened when he hooked it. One of the swans was there on the water, and followed the fish up when it was hooked, and when he drew it to land the swan came out and dashed at and attacked him with the greatest fury. He had a good deal of trouble to beat her off! 'Oh, what a pity!' cried the lady. 'You have killed the poor swan's friend!' From that time the swan was more unhappy than ever; the sight of it became positively painful to my compassionate friends, and by-and-by hearing of an acquaintance in another part of the country who wanted a swan they sent it to him.

⤷ Night, and the Woods, and You

Rupert Brooke (1887–1915) excelled at sensitive observations of natural things – in his poem 'The Voice', from Poems *(1911), he ruefully remembers when he chose the wrong companion.*

Safe in the magic of my woods
   I lay, and watched the dying light.
Faint in the pale high solitudes,
   And washed with rain and veiled by night,

Silver and blue and green were showing.
   And the dark woods grew darker still;
And birds were hushed; and peace was growing;
   And quietness crept up the hill;

And no wind was blowing

And I knew
That this was the hour of knowing,
And the night and the woods and you
Were one together, and I should find
Soon in the silence the hidden key
Of all that had hurt and puzzled me –
Why you were you, and the night was kind,
And the woods were part of the heart of me.

And there I waited breathlessly,
Alone; and slowly the holy three,
The three that I loved, together grew
One, in the hour of knowing,
Night, and the woods, and you –

And suddenly
There was an uproar in my woods,

The noise of a fool in mock distress,
Crashing and laughing and blindly going,
Of ignorant feet and a swishing dress,
And a Voice profaning the solitudes.

The spell was broken, the key denied me
And at length your flat clear voice beside me
Mouthed cheerful clear flat platitudes.

You came and quacked beside me in the wood.
You said, 'The view from here is very good!'
You said, 'It's nice to be alone a bit!'
And, 'How the days are drawing out!' you said.
You said, 'The sunset's pretty, isn't it?'

.   .   .   .   .

By God, I wished that you were dead!

✍ A Love Letter

*Stefana Stevens (1879–1972) based Matravers, the nature-loving hero of her 1916 novel –*And What Happened, *on the young Arthur Ransome (1884 1967) whom she knew in London ten years earlier. The letter sent to his latest love with a box of presents perfectly conveyed Ransome's unique brand of romantic pragmatism and love of country things.*

Moss for the smell. If I was asked what romance smells of, I should say three things – moss on a wet day, a tarred rope on a sunny day, and wood-smoke at all times. That for one of your senses, then. Primroses and the rest for touch – they are fresher and sweeter than those the flower-women sell. I picked them this morning before breakfast. The eggs to remind you of country hedges and what all good birds are about just now. I wish I could send you a little of the concert they favour me with every morning. The plovers' eggs will please Nico, who is greedy. I found them on the moor between here and Dykeham after carefully watching a plover to see where it came to earth. They are hard-boiled. The watercresses were sold to me by a gypsy five minutes ago. The stone is the most valuable thing in the box. Don't ever let it pass out of your possession. It is very rare to find a black kidney-shaped stone, and is one of the luckiest talismans one can possibly possess. I've been looking for one for years. When will you marry me?

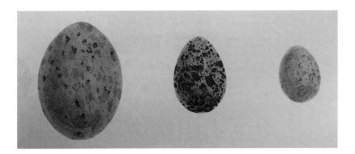

ᘒ Jonah and the Apes

Aldous Huxley (1894–1963), poet, novelist and humanist thinker, wrote these two satirical verses, a sonnet on biblical truth, and five quatrains on evolution, in Leda and Other Poems *(1920).*

Jonah

A cream of phosphorescent light
Floats on the wash that to and fro
Slides round his feet – enough to show
Many a pendulous stalactite
Of naked mucus, whorls and wreaths
And huge festoons of mottled tripes
And smaller palpitating pipes
Through which a yeasty liquor seethes.

Seated upon the convex mound
Of one vast kidney, Jonah prays
And sings his canticles and hymns,
Making the hollow vault resound
God's goodness and mysterious ways.
Till the great fish spouts music as he swims.

First Philosopher's Song

A poor degenerate from the ape,
Whose hands are four, whose tail's a limb,
I contemplate my flaccid shape
And know I may not rival him,

Save with my mind – a nimbler beast
Possessing a thousand sinewy tails,
A thousand hands, with which it scales.
Greedy of luscious truth, the greased

Poles and the coco palms of thought,
Threads easily through the mangrove maze
Of metaphysics, walks the taut
Frail dangerous liana ways

That link across wide gulfs remote
Analogies between tree and tree;
Outruns the hare, outhops the goat;
Mind fabulous, mind sublime and free!

But oh, the sound of simian mirth!
Mind, issued from the monkey's womb.
Is still umbilical to earth,
Earth its home and earth its tomb.

✑ A Very Spiritual Look

George Orwell (1903–1950) had a keen interest in natural things, revelling in wandering by the Thames and living in a remote retreat in Jura. This extract is from 'Some Thoughts on the Common Toad', which appeared in The Tribune *(12 April, 1946).*

Before the swallow, before the daffodil, and not much later than the snowdrop, the common toad salutes the coming of spring after his own fashion, which is to emerge from a hole in the ground, where he has lain buried since the previous autumn, and crawl as rapidly as possible towards the nearest suitable patch of water. Something – some kind of shudder in the earth, or perhaps merely a rise of a few degrees in the temperature – has told him that it is time to wake up: though a few toads appear to sleep the clock round and miss out a year from time to time – at any rate, I have more than once dug them up, alive and apparently well, in the middle of the summer.

At this period, after his long fast, the toad has a very spiritual look, like a strict Anglo-Catholic towards the end of Lent. His movements are languid but purposeful, his body is shrunken, and by contrast his eyes look abnormally large. This allows one to notice what one might not at another time, that a toad has about the most beautiful eye of any living creature. It is like gold, or more exactly it is like the golden-coloured semi-precious stone which one sometimes sees in signet rings, and which I think is called a chrysoberyl.

For a few days after getting into the water the toad concentrates on building up his strength by eating small insects. Presently he has swollen to his normal size again, and then he goes through a phase of intense sexiness. All he knows, at least if he is a male toad, is that he wants to get his arms round something, and if you offer him a stick, or even your finger, he will cling to it with surprising strength and take a long time to discover that it is not a female toad. Frequently one comes upon shapeless masses of ten or twenty toads rolling over

The little husband stands in some awe of his portly spouse

and over in the water, one clinging to another without distinction of sex. By degrees, however, they sort themselves out into couples, with the male duly sitting on the female's back. You can now distinguish males from females, because the male is smaller, darker and sits on top, with his arms tightly clasped round the female's neck. After a day or two the spawn is laid in long strings which wind themselves in and out of the reeds and soon become invisible. A few more weeks, and the water is alive with masses of tiny tadpoles which rapidly grow larger, sprout hind-legs, then forelegs, then shed their tails: and finally, about the middle of the summer, the new generation of toads, smaller than one's thumb-nail but perfect in every particular, crawl out of the water to begin the game anew.

Deep Thinking

And this our life, exempt from public haunt,
Finds tongues in trees, books in the running brooks,
Sermons in stones, and good in everything.
I would not change it.

William Shakespeare, *As You Like It*, **Act II, Scene 1**

ϵ϶ Mornings are Mysteries

The Welsh metaphysical poet Henry Vaughan (1621–1695) had an acute feeling for the relationship between nature and God; these lines come from 'Rules and Lessons', one of the poems in Silex Scintillans *(1650), which means 'The Fiery Flint'.*

Never sleep with sun up… sleep doth sins glut,
And heaven's gate opens when this world's is shut.
Mornings are mysteries; the first world's youth,
Man's resurrection and the future's bud
Shroud in their births; the crown of life, light, truth
Is styled their star, the stone, and hidden food…

Observe God in His works; here fountains flow,
Birds sing, beasts feed, fish leap, and th' Earth stands fast;
Above are restless motions, running lights.
Vast circling azure, giddy clouds, days, nights.

When seasons change, then lay before thine eyes
His wondrous method; mark the various scenes
In heav'n; hail, thunder, rainbows, snow, and ice,
Calms, tempests, light, and darkness, by His means;
Thou canst not miss His praise; each tree, herb, flower,
Are shadows of His wisdom, and His pow'r.

Like its Own Tear

Andrew Marvell (1621–1678) wrote 'On a Drop of Dew' as a delicate and elaborate conceit in which a dewdrop on a rose is likened to the tear of a soul in search of God.

See how the orient dew,
Shed from the bosom of the morn
  Into the blowing roses,
Yet careless of its mansion new,
For the clear region where 'twas born
  Round in itself incloses:
  And in its little globe's extent,
Frames as it can its native element.
  How it the purple flow'r does slight,
    Scarce touching where it lies,
  But gazing back upon the skies,
    Shines with a mournful light,
      Like its own tear,
Because so long divided from the sphere.
  Restless it rolls and unsecure,
    Trembling lest it grow impure,
  Till the warm sun pity its pain,
And to the skies exhale it back again.
  So the soul, that drop, that ray
Of the clear fountain of eternal day,
Could it within the human flow'r be seen,
  Remembering still its former height,
  Shuns the sweet leaves and blossoms green,
  And recollecting its own light,
Does, in its pure and circling thoughts, express
The greater heaven in an heaven less.
  In how coy a figure wound,

Every way it turns away:
So the world excluding round,
Yet receiving in the day,
Dark beneath, but bright above,
Here disdaining, there in love.
How loose and easy hence to go,
How girt and ready to ascend,
Moving but on a point below,
It all about does upwards bend.
Such did the manna's sacred dew distil,
White and entire, though congealed and chill,
Congealed on earth: but does, dissolving, run
Into the glories of th' almighty sun.

ᐇ Vast Chain of Being

Alexander Pope (1688–1744) won instant acclaim for his Essay on Man *(1734). This passage outlines the ancient but still current idea of necessary links between all natural phenomena.*

See, through this air, this ocean, and this earth,
All matter quick, and bursting into birth.
Above, how high, progressive life may go!
Around, how wide! how deep extend below!
Vast chain of being, which from God began,
Natures ethereal, human, angel, man,
Beast, bird, fish, insect! what no eye can see,
No glass can reach! from infinite to thee,
From thee to nothing! – On superior pow'rs
Were we to press, inferior might on ours:
Or in the full creation leave a void,
Where, one step broken, the great scale's destroy'd:
From nature's chain whatever link you strike,
Tenth or ten thousandth, breaks the chain alike.

And, if each system in gradation roll
Alike essential to th' amazing whole,
The least confusion but in one, not all
That system only, but the whole must fall.
Let earth unbalanc'd from her orbit fly,
Planets and suns run lawless through the sky;
Let ruling angels from their spheres be hurl'd,
Being on being wreck'd, and world on world;
Heav'n's whole foundations to their centre nod,
And nature tremble to the throne of God.
All this dread order break – for whom? for thee?
Vile worm! – Oh madness, pride, impiety!

◌ I Have Nothing to Report

Ryokan Taigu (1758–1831) was a Zen Buddhist monk with a great sense of humour, famous for his poetry, his calligraphy and his eccentricities.

My hut lies in the middle of a dense forest;
Every year the green ivy grows longer.
No news of the affairs of men,
Only the occasional song of a woodcutter.
The sun shines and I mend my robe;
When the moon comes out I read Buddhist poems.
I have nothing to report, my friends.
If you want to find the meaning,
Stop chasing after so many things.

❧ The Sense of Magnitude

Samuel Taylor Coleridge's son Hartley (1846–1920) presented some of his father's greatest writing on Nature in Anima Poetae *(1895), his edition of his father's notebooks. This passage was written while Coleridge was living at Greta Hall, Keswick between 1800 and 1803.*

Tuesday, Jan. 15, 1805

This evening there was the most perfect and the brightest halo circling the roundest and brightest moon I ever beheld. So bright was the halo, so compact, so entire a circle, that it gave the whole of its area, the moon itself included, the appearance of a solid opaque body, an enormous planet. It was as if this planet had a circular trough of some light-reflecting fluid for its rim (that is the halo) and its centre (that is the moon) a small circular basin of some fluid that still more copiously reflected, or that even emitted light; and as if the interspatial area were somewhat equally substantial but sullen.

Thence I have found occasion to meditate on the nature of the sense of magnitude and its absolute dependence on the idea of substance; the consequent difference between magnitude and spaciousness, the dependence of the idea on double-touch, and thence to evolve all our feelings and ideas of magnitude, magnitudinal sublimity, &c., from a scale of our own bodies.

For why, if form constituted the sense, that is, if it were pure vision, as a perceptive sense abstracted from feeling in the organ of vision, why do I seek for mountains, when in the flattest countries the clouds present so many and so much more romantic and spacious forms, and the coal-fire so many, so much more varied and lovely forms? And whence arises the pleasure from musing on the latter? Do I not, more or less consciously, fancy myself a Lilliputian to whom these would be mountains, and so, by this factitious scale, make them mountains, my pleasure being consequently playful, a voluntary poem in hieroglyphics or picture-writing – 'phantoms of sublimity', which I continue to know to be phantoms? And form itself, is not its main agency exerted in individualising the thing, making it this and that, and thereby facilitating the shadowy measurement of it by the scale of my own body?

Yon long, not unvaried, ridge of hills, that runs out of sight each way, it is spacious, and the pleasure derivable from it is from its running, its motion, its assimilation to action; and here the scale is taken from my life and soul, and not from my body. Space is the Hebrew name for God, and it is the most perfect image of soul, pure soul, being to us nothing but unresisted action. Whenever action is resisted, limitation begins—and limitation is the first constituent of body—the more omnipresent it is in a given space, the more that space is body or matter—and thus all body necessarily presupposes soul, inasmuch as all resistance presupposes action. Magnitude, therefore, is the intimate blending, the most perfect union, through its whole sphere, in every minutest part of it, of action and resistance to action. It is spaciousness in which space is filled up—that is, as we well say, transmitted by incorporate accession, not destroyed. In all limited things, that is, in all forms, it is at least fantastically stopped, and, thus, from the positive grasp to the mountain, from the mountain to the cloud, from the cloud to the blue depth of sky, which, as on the top of Etna, in a serene atmosphere, seems to go behind the sun, all is graduation, that precludes division, indeed, but not distinction.

↪ The Measure of the Year

John Keats (1795–1821) wrote 'The Human Seasons' at Teignmouth in March 1818 and enclosed it in a letter to his Oxford contemporary Benjamin Bailey; it was first published in Leigh Hunt's Literary Pocket-book *(1819).*

Four Seasons fill the measure of the year;
There are four seasons in the mind of man:
He has his lusty Spring, when fancy clear
Takes in all beauty with an easy span:
He has his Summer, when luxuriously
Spring's honied cud of youthful thought he loves
To ruminate, and by such dreaming high
Is nearest unto heaven: quiet coves
His soul has in its Autumn, when his wings
He furleth close; contented so to look
On mists in idleness—to let fair things
Pass by unheeded as a threshold brook.
He has his Winter too of pale misfeature,
Or else he would forego his mortal nature.

❧ Some Blessed Hope

Thomas Hardy could find hope, for all his professed atheism, in observing the natural world, as in 'The Darkling Thrush'. It first appeared in The Graphic *on 29 December 1900, and was originally called 'The Century's End, 1900'.*

I leant upon a coppice gate
    When Frost was spectre-grey,
And Winter's dregs made desolate
    The weakening eye of day.
The tangled bine-stems scored the sky
    Like strings of broken lyres,
And all mankind that haunted nigh
    Had sought their household fires.

The land's sharp features seemed to be
    The Century's corpse outleant,
His crypt the cloudy canopy,
    The wind his death-lament.
The ancient pulse of germ and birth
    Was shrunken hard and dry,
And every spirit upon earth
    Seemed fervourless as I.

At once a voice arose among
    The bleak twigs overhead
In a full-hearted evensong
    Of joy illimited;
An aged thrush, frail, gaunt, and small,
    In blast-beruffled plume,
Had chosen thus to fling his soul
    Upon the growing gloom.

So little cause for carolings
    Of such ecstatic sound
Was written on terrestrial things
    Afar or nigh around,
That I could think there trembled through
    His happy good-night air
Some blessed Hope, whereof he knew
    And I was unaware.

ᘓ Away Grief's Gasping

Gerard Manley Hopkins (1844–1889) wrote 'That Nature is a Heraclitean Fire and of the comfort of the Resurrection', Poems (1918), when he was on the road to recovery and hope after writing his so called 'terrible' sonnets.

Cloud-Puffball, torn tufts, tossed pillows | flaunt forth, then chevy
   on an air-built thoroughfare: heaven-roysterers, in gay-gangs |
   they throng; they glitter in marches.
Down roughcast, down dazzling whitewash, | wherever an elm arches,
Shivelights and shadowtackle in long | lashes lace, lance, and pair.
Delightfully the bright wind boisterous | ropes, wrestles, beats
   earth bare
Of yestertempest's creases; in pool and rut peel parches
Squandering ooze to squeezed | dough, crust, dust; stanches, starches
Squadroned masks and manmarks | treadmire toil there
Footfretted in it. Million-fuelèd, | nature's bonfire burns on.
But quench her bonniest, dearest | to her, her clearest-selvèd spark
Man, how fast his firedint, | his mark on mind, is gone!
Both are in an unfathomable, all is in an enormous dark
Drowned. O pity and indig | nation! Manshape, that shone
Sheer off, disseveral, a star, | death blots black out; nor mark
Is any of him at all so stark
But vastness blurs and time | beats level. Enough! the
   Resurrection,
A heart's-clarion! Away grief's gasping, | joyless days, dejection.
   Across my foundering deck shone
A beacon, an eternal beam. | Flesh fade, and mortal trash
Fall to the residuary worm; | world's wildfire, leave but ash: In a
   flash, at a trumpet crash,
I am all at once what Christ is, | since he was what I am, and
This Jack, joke, poor potsherd, | patch, matchwood, immortal
   diamond, Is immortal diamond.

❧ In the Highlands

Robert Louis Stevenson (1850–1894) wrote this wistful homage to his home-land just before his death. It appeared in Songs of Travel *(1896).*

In the highlands, in the country places,
Where the old plain men have rosy faces,
And the young fair maidens
Quiet eyes;
Where essential silence cheers and blesses,
And for ever in the hill-recesses
Her more lovely music
Broods and dies.

O to mount again where erst I haunted;
Where the old red hills are bird-enchanted,

And the low green meadows
Bright with sward;
And when even dies, the million-tinted,
And the night has come, and planets glinted,
Lo, the valley hollow
Lamp-bestarred!

O to dream, O to awake and wander
There, and with delight to take and render,
Through the trance of silence,
Quiet breath;
Lo! for there, among the flowers and grasses,
Only the mightier movement sounds and passes;
Only winds and rivers,
Life and death.

✍ Is There Anything Beyond?

Rupert Brooke (1887–1915) wrote 'Heaven' as a tongue-in-cheek satire on the search for the meaning of life. It was published in 1914 and Other Poems *(1915).*

Fish (fly-replete, in depth of June,
Dawdling away their wat'ry noon)
Ponder deep wisdom, dark or clear,
Each secret fishy hope or fear.
Fish say, they have their Stream and Pond;
But is there anything Beyond?
This life cannot be All, they swear,
For how unpleasant, if it were!
One may not doubt that, somehow, Good
Shall come of Water and of Mud;
And, sure, the reverent eye must see
A Purpose in Liquidity.
We darkly know, by Faith we cry,
The future is not Wholly Dry.
Mud unto mud! – Death eddies near –
Not here the appointed End, not here!
But somewhere, beyond Space and Time.
Is wetter water, slimier slime!
And there (they trust) there swimmeth One
Who swam ere rivers were begun,
Immense, of fishy form and mind,
Squamous, omnipotent, and kind;
And under that Almighty Fin,
The littlest fish may enter in.
Oh! never fly conceals a hook,
Fish say, in the Eternal Brook,
But more than mundane weeds are there,

And mud, celestially fair;
Fat caterpillars drift around,
And Paradisal grubs are found;
Unfading moths, immortal flies,
And the worm that never dies.
And in that Heaven of all their wish,
There shall be no more land, say fish.

❧ Nothing But Life

Virginia Woolf (1882–1941) wrote the unexpectedly optimistic title essay of her collections Death of a Moth *(1942) shortly before she committed suicide: it is full of admiration for a tiny being's energetic determination to survive.*

Moths that fly by day are not properly to be called moths; they do not excite that pleasant sense of dark autumn nights and ivy-blossom which the commonest yellow-underwing asleep in the shadow of the curtain never fails to rouse in us. They are hybrid creatures, neither gay like butterflies nor sombre like their own species. Nevertheless the present specimen, with his narrow hay-coloured wings, fringed with a tassel of the same colour, seemed to be content with life. It was a pleasant morning, mid-September, mild, benignant, yet with a keener breath than that of the summer months. The plough was already scoring the field opposite the window, and where the share had been, the earth was pressed flat and gleamed with moisture. Such vigour came rolling in from the fields and the down beyond that it was difficult to keep the eyes strictly turned upon the book. The rooks too were keeping one of their annual festivities; soaring round the tree tops until it looked as if a vast net with thousands of black knots in it had been cast up into the air; which, after a few moments sank slowly down upon the trees until every twig seemed to have a knot at the end of it. Then, suddenly, the net would be thrown into the air again in a wider circle this time, with the utmost clamour and vociferation, as though to be thrown into the air and settle slowly down upon the treetops were a tremendously exciting experience.

The same energy which inspired the rooks, the ploughmen, the horses, and even, it seemed, the lean bare-backed downs, sent the moth fluttering from side to side of his square of the window-pane. One could not help watching him. One was, indeed, conscious of a queer feeling of pity for him. The possibilities of pleasure seemed that morning so enormous and so various that to have only a moth's part in life, and a day moth's at that, appeared a hard fate, and his zest in enjoying his meagre opportunities to the full, pathetic. He flew vigorously to one corner of his compartment, and, after waiting there a second, flew across to the other. What remained for him but to fly to a third corner and then to a fourth? That was all he could do, in spite of the size of the downs, the width of the sky, the far-off smoke of houses, and the romantic voice, now and then, of a steamer out at sea. What he could do he did. Watching him, it seemed as if a fibre, very thin but pure, of the enormous energy of the world had been thrust into his frail and diminutive body. As often as he crossed the pane, I could fancy that a thread of vital light became visible. He was little or nothing but life.

❧ Wildness is Salvation

Aldo Leopold (1887–1948) was born in Iowa and grew up loving outdoor life. He is now famous as a pioneer of environmental ethics, and his Sand County Almanac *(1949), published just after his death, has sold millions of copies. This extract from a chapter called 'Thinking Like a Mountain' shows why.*

A deep chesty bawl echoes from rimrock to rimrock, rolls down the mountain, and fades into the far blackness of the night. It is an outburst of wild defiant sorrow, and of contempt for all the adversities of the world. Every living thing (and perhaps many a dead one as well) pays heed to that call. To the deer it is a reminder of the way of all flesh, to the pine a forecast of midnight scuffles and of blood upon the snow, to the coyote a promise of gleanings to come, to the cowman a threat of red ink at the bank, to the hunter a challenge of fang against bullet. Yet behind these obvious and immediate hopes and fears there lies a deeper meaning, known only to the mountain itself...

My own conviction on this score dates from the day I saw a wolf die. We were eating lunch on a high rimrock, at the foot of which a turbulent river elbowed its way. We saw what we thought was a doe fording the torrent, her breast awash in white water. When she climbed the bank toward us and shook out her tail, we realized our error: it was a wolf. A half-dozen others, evidently grown pups, sprang from the willows and all joined in a welcoming melee of wagging tails and playful maulings. What was literally a pile of wolves writhed and tumbled in the center of an open flat at the foot of our rimrock.

In those days we had never heard of passing up a chance to kill a wolf. In a second we were pumping lead into the pack, but with more excitement than accuracy ... When our rifles were empty, the old wolf was down, and a pup was dragging a leg into impassable slide-rocks.

We reached the old wolf in time to watch a fierce green fire dying in her eyes. I realized then, and have known ever since, that there was something new to me in those eyes - something known only to her and to the mountain. I was young then, and full of trigger-itch; I thought that because fewer wolves meant more deer, that no wolves would mean hunters' paradise. But after seeing the green fire die, I sensed that neither the wolf nor the mountain agreed with such a view.

Since then I have lived to see state after state extirpate its wolves. I have watched the face of many a newly wolfless mountain, and seen the south-facing slopes wrinkle with a maze of new deer trails. I have seen every edible bush and seedling browsed, first to anaemic desuetude, and then to death. I have seen every edible tree defoliated to the height of a saddlehorn. Such a mountain looks as if someone had given God a new pruning shears, and forbidden Him all other exercise. In the end the starved bones of the hoped-for deer herd, dead of its own too-much, bleach with the bones of the dead sage, or moulder under the high-lined junipers.

I now suspect that just as a deer herd lives in mortal fear of its wolves, so does a mountain live in mortal fear of its deer. And perhaps with better cause, for while a buck pulled down by wolves can be replaced in two or three years, a range pulled down by too many deer may fail of replacement in as many decades. So also with cows. The cowman who cleans his range of wolves does not realize that he is taking over the wolf's job of trimming the herd to fit the range. He has not learned to think like a mountain. Hence we have dustbowls, and rivers washing the future into the sea.

We all strive for safety, prosperity, comfort, long life, and dullness. The deer strives with his supple legs, the cowman with trap and poison, the statesman with pen, the most of us with machines, votes, and dollars, but it all comes to the same thing: peace in our time. A measure of success in this is all well enough, and perhaps is a requisite to objective thinking, but too much safety seems to yield only danger in the long run. Perhaps this is behind Thoreau's dictum: In wildness is the salvation of the world. Perhaps this is the hidden meaning in the howl of the wolf, long known among mountains, but seldom perceived among men.

⮑ Listening and Watching

Chet Raymo (b. 1936) is a naturalist and a physicist who describes himself in his blog as a 'Religious Naturalist'. This passage is from The Soul of the Night – An Astronomical Pilgrimage *(1985).*

I am a child of the Milky Way. The night is my mother. I am made of the dust of stars. Every atom in my body was forged in a star. When the universe exploded into being, already the bird longed for the wood and the fish for the pool. When the first galaxies fell into luminous clumps, already matter was struggling toward consciousness. The star clouds of Sagittarius are a burning bush. If there is a voice in Sagittarius, I'd be a fool not to listen. If God's voice in the night is a scrawny cry, then I'll prick up my ears. If night's faint lights fail to knock me off my feet, then I'll sit back on a dark hillside and wait and watch. A hint here and a trait there. Listening and watching. Waiting, always waiting, for the tingle in the spine.

AFTERWORD

ᵍ Noticing Things

Thomas Hardy, 'Afterwards' (c. 1917).

When the Present has latched its postern behind my tremulous stay,
And the May month flaps its glad green leaves like wings,
Delicate-filmed as new-spun silk, will the neighbours say,
'He was a man who used to notice such things'?

If it be in the dusk when, like an eyelid's soundless blink,
The dewfall-hawk comes crossing the shades to alight
Upon the wind-warped upland thorn, a gazer may think,
'To him this must have been a familiar sight.'

If I pass during some nocturnal blackness, mothy and warm,
When the hedgehog travels furtively over the lawn,
One may say, 'He strove that such innocent creatures should come
    to no harm,
But he could do little for them; and now he is gone.'

If, when hearing that I have been stilled at last, they stand at the door,
Watching the full-starred heavens that winter sees
Will this thought rise on those who will meet my face no more,
'He was one who had an eye for such mysteries'?

And will any say when my bell of quittance is heard in the gloom
And a crossing breeze cuts a pause in its outrollings,
Till they rise again, as they were a new bell's boom,
'He hears it not now, but used to notice such things'?

LIST OF ILLUSTRATIONS

All images are from the collections of the British Library unless otherwise stated

p.2 'The Vale of Festiniog, Merionethshire', engraved by H. Merke after J. Warren, 1814 (Maps K.Top.46.48.d).

p.12 Illustration by Walter Crane. William Morris, *The Story of the Glittering Plain*, Kelmscott Press, 1894 (C.43.f.8).

p.17 Illustration by Gustave Doré. *Milton's Paradise Lost*, 1871–72 (1876.e.29).

p.19 Painting by Barbara Briggs. Eleanor Edith Helme, *The Book of Birds and Beasties*, 1929 (7205.g.21).

p.23 Goredale Scar. Gordon Home, *Yorkshire Dales and Fells*, 1906 (W15/2377).

p.24 Lithograph after Edward Lear. Thomas Bell, *A Monograph of the Testudinata*, 1832–36 (1486.w.2).

p.29 Drawing of ammonites by Robert Hooke (Add.5262, f.152).

p.30 Fay Godwin, *Top Withins near Haworth*, 1977 (FG3017-1).

p.35 'Scoor Eig on the Isle of Eig', drawn and engraved by William Daniell. Richard Ayton, *A Voyage round Great Britain undertaken in the summer of the year 1813...*, 1814–25 (G.7043–6).

p.37 'Entrance into Borrodale', drawn by J. Smith, engraved by Merigot, 1798 (Maps K.Top.10.31.2.a).

p.39 Illustration by Walter Crane. William Morris, *The Story of the Glittering Plain*, Kelmscott Press, 1894 (C.43.f.8).

p.40 Illustration by Walter Crane. William Morris, *The Story of the Glittering Plain*, Kelmscott Press, 1894 (C.43.f.8).

p.44 Fay Godwin, *Moonlight, Avebury*, part of the Ridgeway Series, 1974 (FG1672-2-31a).

p.50 Mountain Hare (winter). Archibald Thorburn, *British Mammals*, 1920–21 (L.R.32.b.8).

p.52 Nimbus – or rain cloud. Charles F. Blunt, *The Beauty of the Heavens*, 1840 (717.g.4).

p.55 November. James Thomson, *The Seasons*, 1857 (C.108.u.26).

p.57 Miniature of a hunting party. Cocharellli treatise, *c.* 1330–40 (Egerton 3127, f.1v).

p.189 Plovers eggs. S. L. Mosley, *A History of British birds, their nests and eggs*, 1884–92 (RB.23.a.34426).

p.193 Illustration by J. A. Shepherd. Marcus Woodward, *In Nature's Ways: a book for all young lovers of Nature, being an introduction to Gilbert White's 'Natural History of Selborne'*, 1914 (7003.dg.28).

p.194 'Cataract on the Llugwy', after an original drawing by Philip de Loutherbourg, 1806 (Maps K.Top.46.54.i).

p.198 Pierre Joseph Redoute, *Les Roses*, 1817–24 (450.h.22).

p.200. Full moon. Okada Baikan, *Picture album of plum blossom*, 1808 (16116.d.1).

p.203 Illustration from *Gems from the Poets, illustrated*. The designs by F. A. Lydon. 1858–60 (1347.i.22).

p.205 Song Thrush. Thomas Littleton Powys Lilford, *Coloured figures of the Birds of the British Islands*, 1885–97 (C.194.b.162).

p.208–09 'Loch scene, Argylshire', drawn and engraved by William Daniell. Richard Ayton, *A Voyage round Great Britain undertaken in the summer of the year 1813...*, 1814–25 (G.7043-6).

p.211 Illustration by G. Denholm. Edward Cuming, *British Sport, Past and Present*, 1909 (7904.dd.2).

p.216 A pack of wolves in pursuit of prey, illustration by Friedrich Specht. Carl Vogt, *The Natural History of Animals in word & picture*, 1887–88 (7205.h.5).

INDEX OF AUTHORS

First published in 2016 by
The British Library
96 Euston Road
London NW1 2DT

Cataloguing in Publication Data
A catalogue record for this publication is available from The British Library

ISBN 978 0 7123 5768 5

Introduction © by Christina Hardyment 2016
Text compilation and editorial © by Christina Hardyment 2016

The right of Christina Hardyment to be identified as the Author of this Work has been
asserted by her in accordance with the Copyright Designs and Patents Act 1988.

Designed and typeset by Briony Hartley, Goldust Design
Picture research by Sally Nicholls
Printed in Malta by Gutenberg Press

CREDITS